Now THAT'S COOKIN'®

A collection of recipes from
Successful Farming® magazine and
The Machine Shed Restaurants

When you see
The Machine Shed logo in this
book, you'll know the recipe comes
straight from their kitchens. Try it
at the restaurant, then make it at
home for your family!

 All other recipes in
this book have been
tested by the same food
authorities who approve all recipes
for Better Homes and Gardens®
magazine, a sister publication
to Successful Farming®.

Visit Agriculture Online®, the Web
site of *Successful Farming* magazine, at
www.agriculture.com.

Visit The Machine Shed Restaurants,
part of Heart of America Restaurants
and Inns, at their locations in
Appleton, Wisconsin; Davenport
and Des Moines, Iowa; Rockford,
Illinois; Pewaukee, Wisconsin; and
Lake Elmo, Minnesota; and find them
online at www.machineshed.com.

Now THAT'S
COOKIN'®

Director of Retail Operations: Jan Kay

SUCCESSFUL FARMING®

Editor: Lisa Foust Prater
Art Director: Kathy Grove
New Product Manager: Diana Willits
Administrative Assistant: Brenda Torsky
Photographs: Jay Wilde
Additional photographs provided by
Meredith Corporation and The Machine Shed
Editor-in-Chief: Loren Kruse
Food Editor: Betsy Freese
Publisher: Scott Mortimer

Meredith CORPORATION

MEREDITH PUBLISHING GROUP
President: Jack Griffin
Operations: Doug Olson
Group Publisher: Tom Davis
President and Chief Executive Officer: Stephen M. Lacy
Chairman of the Board: William T. Kerr
In Memoriam: E. T. Meredith III (1933-2003)

Now That's Cookin' (ISBN-978-0-696-23613-6)
is published by Meredith Corporation,
1716 Locust Street, Des Moines, IA 50309-3023.
© Copyright Meredith Corporation 2007.
All rights reserved.

If you have comments or questions about the material
in this book, please write to the New Product Manager,
Successful Farming magazine, Meredith Corporation,
1716 Locust Street, Des Moines, IA 50309-3023,
or e-mail brenda.torsky@meredith.com,
or call 800/274-2361.

Printed in China

Lisa Foust Prater
Editor, *Now That's Cookin'*

For my mom,

the best cook ever,

and all the moms

and dads who put

dinner on the table

every day. – LFP

Food does more than just sustain us. It draws us together as a family, and as a people. At Successful Farming® magazine, we understand that, which is why we have shared recipes with our readers since our first issue in 1902.

Farming has certainly changed since then, but the delicious aroma of a simmering pot roast or bubbling apple pie still brings the family running to the table, just as it did 100 years ago.

The Machine Shed Restaurants also understand how farm families eat. When Mike Whalen opened the first Machine Shed in 1978, he dedicated the business to the American farmer. "That dedication meant we worked hard to have a restaurant that wasn't just farm-themed, but would be something that farmers could be proud of," he says. From peeling their own potatoes to using only the freshest ingredients, that dedication still shows in every meal The Machine Shed serves.

Whether you're a seasoned farmhand or the ultimate city slicker, the recipes in this book will bring comfort and joy to your family. They are organized as complete meals, but of course you can mix and match, and add your own family favorites to ours. So make some dinner, and make some memories!

Enjoy!

Lisa Foust Prater

About Successful Farming®

It all started more than a century ago on the wedding day of Edwin Thomas Meredith. His grandfather's nuptial gift was a fistful of $20 gold pieces that bought the controlling interest in his grandfather's newspaper, *Farmer's Tribune*. A note that said, "Sink or swim" was attached to the debt-laden balance sheet.

It's clear today that E.T. chose to swim. He turned around the fortune of the paper and sold it for a profit. With the proceeds, he decided to publish a journal that met his vision of what a helpful farm publication should be – a service magazine. In October 1902, the first issue of *Successful Farming* magazine was sold to 500 subscribers. By 1914, circulation was over the half-million mark, and Meredith Corporation was on its way to becoming the media powerhouse it is today.

More than 100 years later, *Successful Farming* still provides ideas farm and ranch families can take right to the field, barn, shop, office, home, family or heart, to add value to their lives, businesses and lifestyles.

About The Machine Shed

The Iowa Machine Shed Restaurant got its start in 1978 in rural Davenport, Iowa, with just 100 seats. The location wasn't great and much of the equipment was old (but clean) and broke too often.

Despite being young and green, the restaurant staff's commitment to the American farmer guided them through the early days. Even though money was tight, they were never tempted to take the cheaper route.

Thanks to folks like you, The Machine Shed has been popular from the very start. The original Machine Shed has been expanded and improved many times. Now other Machine Sheds have sprung up across the Midwest. Along the way we have been delighted to receive a bushel basketful of honors from farm groups like the Pork Producers, Turkey Federation and Beef Industry Council. We are constantly striving to live up to those honors in the food we prepare and the service we provide.

Contents

DINNER VS. SUPPER ... 55

Southern Comfort
Cajun-Flavored Catfish, Hush Puppies
The Machine Shed Coleslaw, Fried Green Tomatoes
Southern Black-Eyed Pea Salad, Lemon Pecan Pie

Perfect Pork
The Machine Shed Stuffed Pork Loin with Sage Dressing
Salad with Holiday Dijon Vinaigrette, The Machine Shed Baked Potato Soup
Farm-Style Green Beans, Pine Nut-Parsley Rolls
The Machine Shed Apple Dumpling

Family Classic
The Machine Shed Meatloaf, The Machine Shed Garlic Mashed Potatoes
Basil Peas and Mushrooms, Creamed Corn Casserole
Cranberry Waldorf Salad, Caramelized Upside-Down Pear Ginger Cake

Sit-Down Dinner
The Machine Shed Old-Fashioned Pot Roast
Glorious Greens with Hazelnut Vinaigrette, Herbed Roasted Vegetables
Mama's Dinner Rolls, Raspberry Pear Jam, Grandma's Berry-Apple Pie

Holiday or Any Day
The Machine Shed French Onion Soup, Hazelnut-Crusted Turkey Breast
Cheesy Wild Rice Casserole, Broccoli and Peppers with Walnuts
Maple-Orange Sweet Potatoes and Carrots, Pumpkin Gingerbread Pie

FRONT-PORCH FARE ... 89

Citrus Snack
Ham, Cheese and Fruit Wedges
Citrus-Mint Drink, Chilled Lemony Pea Soup

Keep it Cool
Cool-as-a-Cucumber Chicken Salad
Watermelon-Berry Sorbet, Refreshing Iced Tea

Fresh From the Garden
Fruit Kabobs, All Wrapped Up Chef Salad, Strawberry Iced Tea

Game Day Delight
Brew Pub Pretzels, Chunky Steak Chili
Hot Chocolate by the Bowlful

Cool-Day Warm-Up
Mini Reubens, Hot Fennel Cheese Dip
Ozark Mountain Mulled Cider

MAKE-AHEAD MEALS ... 101

Busy-Morning Breakfast
Heart-Healthy Apple Coffee Cake
Ginger Fruit Compote

TV-Tray Time
Bacon and Tomato Potato Skins, Buffalo-Style Chicken Fingers
Bottled Blue Cheese Dressing and Celery Sticks, PB&J Ice Cream Sandwiches

Tropical Twist
Individual Pineapple Meatloaves, Cooked Wild Rice
Canned or Frozen Peas, Tropical Fruit Cakes

Hot Start, Cool Finish
Chicken and Duck Hunter Stew, Fresh or Frozen Fruit
Decadent French Silk Pie

STATE FAIR FOOD ... 116

Big Taste, Big Fun
Grilled Behemoth Drumsticks, My Fair Ladies Potato Bread
Farm-Fresh Ice Cream, North 40 Berry Pie

Fair Food on a Stick
Corn Dogs with a Kick, Choose-a-Flavor Caramel Apples
Minnesota Fudge Puppies, Lemon-Orange Shakeups

Farmer's Favorite
Pork Chops on a Stick, Best Homemade French Fries
Blueberry Grunt

Blue-Ribbon Fair Meal
Pork Tenderloin Sandwiches, Grilled Corn on the Cob with Herbs
Fresh Strawberry Ice Cream, Mom's Angel Food Cake

State Fair Classic
Spicy Italian Grinder, Italian Doughnuts, Strawberry Italian Ice
Dad's Gooseberry Pie, Caramel Corn

FARM KID FUN ... 136

Chicken Feed Snack Mix, Fruit-Filled Feed Sacks, Moo Juice
Spiral Silos, Pigs Under Wraps, Sugar Cookie Farm Animals
Farmyard Cake, Graham Cracker Barn and Silo

Rising
WITH THE ROOSTER

Farmers get up early. It's in their blood. And there's usually no need for an alarm clock, or even a rooster.

Spend the night on a farm, and you'll hear your hosts stirring in what you are sure is the middle of the night. "Oh, they're just letting the dog out," you'll think. Then, you'll smell bacon frying.

There's work to be done. Hard work. The kind of work that requires some serious fuel. Cold cereal and buttered toast won't cut the mustard. There has to be protein. There has to be something sweet. And because it's so darned early, there absolutely without a doubt has to be coffee.

So rise and shine! Up and at 'em! You're burning daylight! Let's eat!

Sweet beginnings

The Machine Shed Giant Cinnamon Roll

These gigantic, delicious cinnamon rolls are legendary at The Machine Shed Restaurants, and they're perfectly partnered with this savory breakfast casserole. The dreamy citrus fruit salad balances this great start to the day, and the spicy coffee will get their motors running!

The Machine Shed
Giant Cinnamon Rolls

Prep: 35 minutes Rise: 1 hour, 45 minutes
Bake: 35 minutes

10	to 10½ cups all-purpose flour
2	packages active dry yeast
2½	cups milk
1	cup butter
1	cup sugar
2	teaspoons salt
3	eggs
1	teaspoon vanilla
½	cup packed brown sugar
2	tablespoons ground cinnamon
½	cup butter, softened
1	Recipe Butter Cream Icing *(see page 12)*

1. In a very large mixing bowl combine 3½ cups of the flour and the yeast.

2. In a medium saucepan heat milk, 1 cup butter, 1 cup sugar, and salt just until warm (120° to 130°F.) and butter is almost melted, stirring constantly. Add to flour mixture. Add eggs and vanilla. Beat with an electric mixer on low speed for 30 seconds, scraping sides of bowl constantly. Beat on high speed for 3 minutes. Using a wooden spoon, stir in as much of the remaining flour as you can.

3. Turn dough out onto a lightly floured surface. Knead in enough of the remaining flour to make a moderately soft dough that is smooth and elastic (3 to 5 minutes total). Shape into a ball. Place in a greased bowl, turning once. Cover; let rise in a warm place till double (about 1 hour).

4. For filling, combine brown sugar and cinnamon. Grease two 13×9×2-inch baking pans; set aside.

5. Punch dough down. Turn onto a lightly floured surface. Divide dough in half. Cover and let rest for 10 minutes. Roll half of the dough to a 16×12-inch rectangle.

6. Spread dough with half of the softened butter. Sprinkle with half of the brown sugar mixture. Roll up jelly-roll style starting with one of the short sides; pinch edges to seal. Slice roll into six pieces. Arrange dough pieces, cut sides up, in one of the prepared baking pans. Repeat with remaining dough, butter and filling. Makes 12.

Food experts believe that the first cinnamon rolls were probably made in Sri Lanka, where true cinnamon originates. They were likely enjoyed by the ancient Egyptians, Greeks and Romans before moving into Medieval Europe and the rest of the world. Schnecken, a variation on the cinnamon roll, first became popular in America in Germantown, a suburb of Philadelphia, as early as 1680. English immigrants had their own version in the Chelsea bun.

But it wasn't until The Machine Shed Restaurant began serving their gargantuan, gooey, mouth-watering version that the cinnamon roll truly achieved "perfect food" status. And now, you can make them right in your own kitchen.

THE MACHINE SHED
A restaurant honoring the American farmer ®

Orange Dream Fruit Salad

7. Cover and let dough rise in a warm place until nearly double, about 45 minutes. Preheat oven to 350°F.

8. Bake for 35 to 40 minutes or until browned and rolls sound hollow when lightly tapped. Remove rolls from oven. Cool for 1 minute. Carefully invert cinnamon rolls onto a wire rack. Cool slightly. Invert again onto a serving platter. Spread with butter cream icing. Serve warm. Makes 12 rolls.

Nutrition Facts per serving: *744 calories, 28 g total fat, 84 mg cholesterol, 409 mg sodium, 113 g carbohydrate, 4 g dietary fiber, 13 g protein, 37% DV vitamin A, 13% DV calcium, 28% DV iron.*

Butter Cream Icing

In a large bowl beat together ½ cup butter, softened; 3 cups powdered sugar; 1 teaspoon vanilla; and ½ teaspoon salt. Gradually beat in ¼ cup evaporated milk. Beat in enough additional powdered sugar (about 1½ cups) to make a soft spreading consistency. Makes 1¾ cup frosting.

Orange Dream Fruit Salad
Prep: 30 minutes   Chill: 1¼ hours

3   cups seeded, peeled, and chopped mangoes or papayas (3 medium)
4   11-ounce cans mandarin orange sections, drained
3   cups seedless red and/or green grapes, halved
2   8-ounce containers orange-flavored yogurt
1   teaspoon poppy seeds (optional)
2   cups fresh blueberries or strawberries

In a very large bowl, combine the mangoes or papayas, drained oranges, and grapes. In a medium bowl, stir together the yogurt and poppy seeds. Gently stir yogurt mixture into the fruit mixture until combined. Cover and chill up to 6 hours. Stir in blueberries just before serving. Makes 25 servings.

Nutrition facts per serving: *64 calories, 0 g total fat, 0 g saturated fat, 1 mg cholesterol, 14 mg sodium, 15 g carbohydrate, 1 g fiber, 1 g protein, 40% DV Vitamin C, 4% DV calcium, 1% DV iron.*

The Machine Shed
Baked Cheddar Casserole

1⅔ cups purchased chicken gravy
(or use homemade)
1¼ cups shredded Colby cheese
(5 ounces)
1 8-ounce carton dairy sour cream
⅓ cup butter or margarine, melted
1 onion, chopped
½ teaspoon salt
¼ teaspoon ground white pepper
1 32-ounce package frozen hash brown
potatoes, thawed.

1. Lightly grease a 3-quart rectangular baking dish; set aside.

2. In a very large bowl stir together the gravy, cheese, sour cream, butter, onion, salt, and pepper. Add potatoes and mix well.

3. Spoon into prepared dish. Cover and bake in a 350°F. oven for 1 hour or until heated through. Let stand 10 minutes before serving. Makes 12 servings.

Spicy Coffee
Prep: 30 minutes   Chill: 1¼ hours

4 cups brewed coffee
2 inches stick cinnamon
½ teaspoon whole allspice
2 2 × ½-inch strips orange peel
Stick cinnamon (optional)

1. In a medium saucepan combine coffee, 2 inches stick cinnamon, allspice, and orange peel. Bring to boiling; reduce heat. Cover and simmer for 5 minutes.

2. Remove solids from coffee with a slotted spoon. Pour coffee into coffee cups. If desired, garnish with cinnamon sticks. For iced coffee, chill after simmering and pour over ice in tall glasses. Makes 6 (5-ounce) servings.

Nutrition facts per serving: *3 calories, 0 g total fat, 0 mg cholesterol, 3 mg sodium, 0 g carbohydrate, 0 g protein.*

The Machine Shed Baked Cheddar Casserole

The Machine Shed Applesauce Sweet Bread

Bread-basket breakfast

There's something for everyone in this serve-yourself breakfast. Let them choose their favorite breads to go with the easy quiche, and blend custom smoothies with fruits you have on hand.

The Machine Shed Applesauce Sweet Bread

- 3 cups all-purpose flour
- 1½ teaspoons baking soda
- 1 teaspoon salt
- 1 cup butter, softened
- 1½ cups sugar
- 3 eggs
- ¼ cup evaporated milk or milk
- 1 teaspoon vanilla
- 1½ cups applesauce
- 2 tablespoons cinnamon-sugar

1. Grease the bottoms and ½ inch up the sides of two 8×4×2-inch loaf pans; set aside.
2. In a medium bowl stir together flour, soda, and salt; set aside.
3. In a large mixing bowl beat butter with an electric mixer on medium to high speed for 30 seconds. Add sugar and beat until well-combined. Beat in eggs, milk, and vanilla. Beat in applesauce. Beat in flour mixture until combined.
4. Divide mixture between prepared pans. Sprinkle tops of each with cinnamon-sugar. Bake in a 325°F. oven for 60 minutes or until a toothpick inserted near the centers comes out clean. Cool in pans on wire racks for 10 minutes. Remove from pans and cool completely. Makes 2 loaves.

THE MACHINE SHED
A restaurant honoring the American farmer ®

This Applesauce Sweet Bread is a perennial favorite at The Machine Shed Restaurants.

It's served family-style, in a basket with other delicious breads and scrumptious spreads. It's not just for breakfast, though – serve it alongside your favorite lunch or dinner for a touch of sweetness.

Bunch of
Banana Bread

Prep: 15 minutes   Bake: 45 minutes

	Nonstick cooking spray
1½	cups all-purpose flour
1¼	teaspoons baking powder
½	teaspoon baking soda
½	teaspoon ground cinnamon
⅛	teaspoon salt
2	slightly beaten egg whites
1	cup mashed banana (3 medium)
¾	cup sugar
¼	cup cooking oil

1. Lightly coat an 8×4×2-inch loaf pan with cooking spray; set aside. In a medium bowl combine flour, baking powder, baking soda, cinnamon, and salt. Set aside.

2. In a large bowl stir together the egg whites, banana, sugar, and oil. Add flour mixture all at once to banana mixture. Stir just until moistened (the batter should be lumpy). Spoon batter into prepared pan.

3. Bake in a 350°F. oven for 45 to 50 minutes or until a wooden toothpick inserted near the center comes out clean.

4. Cool in pan on a wire rack for 10 minutes. Remove from pan. Cool completely on rack. Wrap and store overnight before slicing. Makes 1 loaf (16 servings).

Nutrition facts per serving: *127 calories, 4 g total fat, 1 g saturated fat, 0 mg cholesterol, 96 mg sodium, 23 g carbohydrate, 1 g fiber, 2 g protein, 2% DV Vitamin C, 2% DV calcium, 3% DV iron.*

Bunch of Banana Bread

Cranberry Twist Bread

Cranberry Twist Bread

Prep: 30 minutes   Rise: 1½ hours
Bake: 25 minutes

- 2¾ to 3 cups all-purpose flour
- 1 package active dry yeast
- ¾ cup milk
- ⅓ cup granulated sugar
- 2 tablespoons butter or margarine
- 1 egg
- ½ cup finely chopped cranberries
- 2 tablespoons finely chopped pecans
- 1½ teaspoons finely shredded orange peel
- ½ teaspoon pumpkin pie spice or apple pie spice
- 1½ teaspoons butter or margarine, melted
- 1 recipe Orange Icing (recipe follows)

1. In a large bowl stir together 1 cup of the flour and the yeast; set aside. In a small saucepan heat and stir milk, 2 tablespoons of the granulated sugar, the 2 tablespoons butter, and ½ teaspoon salt until warm (120°F. to 130°F.). Add milk mixture to flour mixture; add egg. Beat with an electric mixer on low to medium speed for 30 seconds, scraping sides of bowl. Beat on high speed for 3 minutes. Stir in as much of the remaining flour as you can.

2. Turn out dough onto a floured surface. Knead in enough remaining flour to make a soft dough that is smooth and elastic (3 to 5 minutes total). Shape dough into a ball. Place in a lightly greased bowl; turn once. Cover; let rise in a warm place until double (1 to 1½ hours).

3. Meanwhile, for filling, in a small bowl stir together cranberries, remaining sugar, pecans, orange peel, and spice; set aside.

4. Punch down dough. Turn out onto lightly floured surface. Cover; let rest 10 minutes. Grease a baking sheet. Roll dough into a 14×10-inch rectangle. Brush with melted butter. Spread filling over dough. Starting from a long side, roll dough into a spiral. Seal seam. Place seam side down and cut roll in half lengthwise. Place cut sides up, side by side, on prepared baking sheet. Loosely twist halves together, keeping the cut sides up. Pinch ends to seal. Cover; let rise in a warm place until nearly double (about 30 minutes).

5. Bake in a 375°F. oven about 25 minutes or until golden brown (if necessary, cover loosely with foil the last 10 minutes to prevent overbrowning). Remove from baking sheet; cool on a wire rack. Drizzle with Orange Icing. Makes 16 servings.

Orange Icing: Stir together ½ cup sifted powdered sugar and enough orange juice (2 to 3 teaspoons) to make icing of drizzling consistency.

Nutrition facts per serving: *136 calories, 3 g total fat, 2 g saturated fat, 1 g monounsaturated fat, 0 g polyunsaturated fat, 19 mg cholesterol, 102 mg sodium, 24 g carbohydrate, 8 g total sugar, 1 g fiber, 3 g protein, 2% DV Vitamin C, 2% DV calcium, 6% DV iron.*

Shortcut Ham Quiche

Shortcut Ham Quiche

Prep: 15 minutes
Bake: 8 minutes plus 30 minutes

1   8-ounce package
    (8) refrigerated crescent rolls
1   cup diced cooked ham (5 ounces)
4   ounces Havarti dill cheese, shredded
    (1 cup)
2   eggs
1   5-ounce can (⅔ cup) evaporated milk
½   teaspoon Dijon-style mustard
⅓   cup sliced almonds, toasted (optional)

1. Preheat oven to 375°F. Grease a 9-inch pie plate. Unroll crescent rolls and press into bottom and onto side of the prepared pie plate. If desired, mark the edge of the pastry with the tines of a fork. Bake in preheated oven for 8 minutes. Remove from oven.

2. Sprinkle ham and cheese over the pastry. In a small bowl beat eggs with a wire whisk; whisk in evaporated milk and mustard. Pour egg mixture over ham and cheese. Cover edge of pastry with foil. Bake in the 375°F. oven for 30 to 35 minutes or until a knife inserted near the center comes out clean. If desired, sprinkle with almonds. Let stand for 5 minutes before serving. Makes 4 to 6 servings.

Nutrition facts per serving: *471 calories, 32 g total fat, 6 g saturated fat, 172 mg cholesterol, 1152 mg sodium, 27 g carbohydrate, 0 g fiber, 22 g protein.*

Mixed Fruit Smoothies
Start to finish: 10 minutes

2 **bananas, chilled**
⅔ **cup strawberries or mango slices**
1 **12-ounce can grape juice or mango, apricot, strawberry, or other fruit nectar, chilled**
1 **8-ounce carton fat-free yogurt**
1 **tablespoon honey (optional)**
2 **tablespoons ground pistachio nuts (optional)**

In a blender combine bananas, strawberries or mango slices, grape juice or fruit nectar, yogurt, and, if desired, honey. Cover and blend until smooth. Pour into six tall, chilled glasses. If desired, sprinkle with ground pistachio nuts. Makes 6 smoothies.

Note: For two-tone smoothies, make mango smoothies and strawberry smoothies. Transfer to separate pitchers or glass measuring cups. Taking a pitcher or cup in each hand, slowly pour both smoothies at the same time into opposite sides of the glass.

Nutrition facts per serving: 152 calories, 2 g total fat, 0 g saturated fat, 1 mg cholesterol, 50 mg sodium, 47 g carbohydrate, 3 g fiber, 2% DV Vitamin A, 33% DV vitamin C, 14% DV calcium, 5% DV iron.

Mixed Fruit Smoothies

Farmhand flapjacks

Buckwheat Pancakes

Who doesn't love pancakes? Buckwheat makes these cakes hearty enough for a farmhand. Pass the syrup!

Buckwheat Pancakes
Start to finish: 25 minutes

1¼	cups buttermilk or sour milk
3	tablespoons butter or margarine, melted
1	large egg
½	cup all-purpose flour
⅓	cup buckwheat flour
¾	teaspoon baking soda
¼	teaspoon salt
	Maple syrup
	Vegetable cooking spray

1. Whisk buttermilk, butter, and egg together in bowl until blended. Combine flours, soda, and salt in another bowl. Whisk buttermilk mixture into dry ingredients until just blended.

2. Heat large nonstick skillet or griddle over medium-high heat. Grease lightly with vegetable cooking spray. For each pancake, spoon scant ¼ cup of the batter into skillet, spreading batter lightly with back of spoon. Cook until bubbles form on surface of pancakes, about 2 minutes. Turn pancakes over and cook 1 to 2 minutes more. Repeat with remaining batter. Serve with maple syrup. Makes 12 pancakes.

Nutrition facts per serving: *125 calories, 4 g total fat, 2 g saturated fat, 26 mg cholesterol, 160 mg sodium, 20 g carbohydrate, 2 mg calcium.*

TEST KITCHEN TIP: TO MAKE 1¼ CUPS SOUR MILK, PLACE 4 TEASPOONS LEMON JUICE OR VINEGAR IN A 2-CUP GLASS MEASURING CUP. ADD ENOUGH MILK TO MAKE 1¼ CUPS LIQUID; STIR. LET THE MIXTURE STAND FOR 5 MINUTES BEFORE USING IT IN A RECIPE.

Brown Sugar Syrup
Start to finish: 10 minutes

2	cups packed dark brown sugar
1	cup water
1	teaspoon vanilla

In a medium saucepan combine brown sugar and water. Cook and stir over medium-high heat until sugar dissolves. Bring to boiling. Reduce heat and simmer, uncovered, for 5 minutes. Remove from heat. Stir in vanilla. Serve warm or cool. Cover and refrigerate remaining syrup for up to 1 week. Makes 1⅔ cups.

Nutrition facts per serving: *50 calories, 0 g total fat, 0 g saturated fat, 0 mg cholesterol, 4 mg sodium, 13 g carbohydrate, 0 g fiber, 0 g protein, 1% DV iron.*

Blueberry Syrup
Prep: 5 minutes   Cook: 25 minutes

2	cups fresh or frozen blueberries
½	cup water
⅓	cup sugar
2	teaspoons lime juice or lemon juice

In a medium saucepan combine 1 cup of the blueberries, the water, sugar and lime or lemon juice. Cook and stir over medium heat for 2 to 3 minutes or until sugar dissolves. Bring to boiling. Reduce heat and simmer, uncovered, for 15 to 20 minutes or until slightly thickened, stirring occasionally.

Stir in remaining 1 cup blueberries and cook, stirring occasionally, 2 to 3 minutes more or until blueberries become soft. Serve warm. Cover and refrigerate remaining syrup for up to 1 week.

Basil Scrambled Eggs and Corn Bread Toast

Prep: 25 minutes   Bake: 20 minutes
Cool: 15 minutes

1   8-oz. package corn bread mix
1   cup shredded cheddar cheese
½   of a 32-oz. package frozen hash brown potatoes (about 3½ cups)
6   eggs
⅓   cup milk, half-and-half, or light cream
¼   teaspoon salt
    Dash ground black pepper
1   tablespoon butter or margarine
½   cup snipped fresh basil

1. Preheat oven to 400°F. Prepare corn bread mix according to package directions, stirring ½ cup of the cheese into the batter. Spread batter in a greased 8×4-inch loaf pan. Bake 20 minutes or until corn bread is lightly browned and a wooden pick inserted near center comes out clean. Cool corn bread in pan on a wire rack for 10 minutes. Remove corn bread from pan; cool completely.

2. In a large skillet, prepare hash brown potatoes according to package directions. Sprinkle potatoes with remaining ½ cup cheese during last 2 minutes of cooking. Set aside; keep warm.

3. Preheat oven to 300°F. Slice corn bread loaf into 8 slices (about 1-inch). Lay slices on a baking sheet. Place in oven to warm. Meanwhile, in a medium bowl beat together eggs, milk, salt, and pepper with a wire whisk just until combined. In a large skillet melt butter over medium heat and pour in egg mixture. Cook over medium heat, without stirring, until eggs begin to set on the bottom and around the edge.

4. With a spatula or large spoon, lift and fold the partially cooked egg mixture to let the uncooked portion flow underneath. Cook over medium heat for 2 to 3 minutes or until egg mixture is cooked through but still glossy and moist. Remove from heat immediately.

5. To serve, place 2 slices of corn bread on each of four plates. Divide scrambled eggs and hash browns among the plates. Sprinkle eggs and hash browns with fresh basil. Makes 4 servings.

Nutrition Facts per serving: *635 calories, 31 g total fat, 11 g saturated fat, 396 mg cholesterol, 960 mg sodium, 66 g carbohydrate., 2 g dietary fiber, 26 g protein, 21% DV Vitamin A, 17% DV Vitamin C, 38% DV calcium, 23% DV iron.*

Basil Scrambled Eggs and Corn Bread Toast

Fruit with Minted Yogurt

Spiced Orange Mocha
Prep: 15 minutes

1   medium orange
7   whole cloves
2   cups water
2   cups milk
½   cup packed brown sugar
¼   cup unsweetened cocoa powder
2   tablespoons instant coffee crystals
¼   teaspoon rum extract
2   inches stick cinnamon

1. Using a vegetable peeler or sharp knife, remove peel from orange; set aside. Squeeze juice from orange; add water, if necessary, to equal ⅓ cup. Set aside.

2. For spice bag, place orange peel, cinnamon, and cloves in a double layer square of 100% cotton cheesecloth. Bring up corners; tie with string.

3. In a large saucepan combine orange juice, spice bag, water, milk, brown sugar, cocoa powder, and coffee crystals. Bring to boiling; remove from heat. Cover and let stand for 10 minutes. Remove spice bag. Stir in rum extract. Makes 6 (6-ounce) servings.

Nutrition facts per serving: *136 calories, 2 g total fat, 6 mg cholesterol, 51 mg sodium, 26 g carbohydrate, 0 g fiber, 4 g protein, 5% DV Vitamin A, 14% DV Vitamin C, 13% DV calcium, 6% DV iron.*

Fruit with Minted Yogurt
Prep: 15 minutes

1   16-ounce carton plain low-fat yogurt
3   tablespoons honey
2   tablespoons snipped fresh mint
4   medium plums, pitted and thinly sliced (about 3 cups)
3   cups assorted berries (such as blueberries, raspberries, and strawberries)
     Fresh mint sprigs (optional)

In a small bowl stir together yogurt, honey, and snipped mint. Cover and refrigerate until ready to serve. In a medium bowl combine plums and berries. Divide fruit among six individual dessert bowls. Spoon minted yogurt on top. Garnish with fresh mint sprigs, if desired. Makes 6 servings.

Nutrition facts per serving: *144 calories, 1 g total fat, 0 g saturated fat, 1 mg cholesterol, 56 mg sodium, 31 g carbohydrate, 3 g fiber, 5 g protein, 52% DV Vitamin C, 11% DV calcium, 5% DV iron.*

Spiced Orange Mocha

23

Good Morning Oatmeal

Fuel for the day

These recipes turn ordinary oatmeal and eggs into a special breakfast that will get everyone up and moving.

What a perfect way to tell your family, "Good morning!"

Good Morning Oatmeal

Prep: 10 minutes   Cook: 30 minutes

1¾ cups apple juice
1   7-ounce package mixed dried fruit bits
⅓   cup packed brown sugar
3   inches stick cinnamon or ½ teaspoon ground cinnamon
2   medium pears, cored and chopped
5   cups water (or 2½ cups water and 2½ cups milk)
½   teaspoon salt
3   cups quick-cooking oats
2   6-ounces containers vanilla yogurt
1   cup granola

In saucepan combine juice, fruit bits, sugar, and cinnamon. Bring to boiling. Reduce heat; simmer, covered, 20 minutes. Add pears. Cook, covered, 10 minutes. Cool; remove cinnamon stick. Drain, discard liquid. In saucepan bring water and salt to boiling. Add oats. Reduce heat to medium; cook about 1 minute, stirring occasionally. To serve, top with fruit mixture, yogurt, and granola. Makes 8 servings.

Nutrition facts per serving: *357 calories, 5 g total fat, 2 g saturated fat, 2 g monounsaturated fat, 1 g polyunsaturated fat, 2 mg cholesterol, 204 mg sodium, 74 g carbohydrate, 28 g total sugar, 5 g fiber, 8 g protein, 5% DV Vitamin C, 11% DV calcium, 13% DV iron.*

The Machine Shed Farmer's Benedict Breakfast

8 eggs
1 recipe Hollandaise Sauce (right)
4 English muffins, split and toasted
   Butter, softened
8 slices Canadian-style bacon
   Cooked hash brown potatoes

1. Lightly grease a large skillet. Add water to half-fill the skillet. Bring water to boiling; reduce heat to simmering. Break one of the eggs into a measuring cup. Carefully slide egg into simmering water, holding the lip of the cup as close to the water as possible. Repeat with remaining eggs, allowing each egg an equal amount of space.

2. Simmer eggs, uncovered, for 3 to 5 minutes or until the whites are completely set and yolks begin to thicken but are not hard. Remove with a slotted spoon and place in a large pan of warm water to keep them warm. Prepare Hollandaise Sauce.

3. Spread muffin halves with butter. Top each with a slice of bacon and then an egg. Spoon sauce over each. Makes 8 servings.

Hollandaise Sauce

1 cup unsalted butter
6 egg yolks, lightly beaten
2 tablespoons lemon juice
2 tablespoons water
   Salt
   Ground white pepper

1. Cut the butter into six pieces and bring it to room temperature; allow about 45 minutes.

2. In the top of double boiler combine the egg yolks, lemon juice, and water. Add a piece of the butter. Place over gently boiling water (upper pan should not touch water). Cook, stirring rapidly with a whisk, until butter melts and sauce begins to thicken. Sauce may appear to curdle at this point, but will smooth out when remaining butter is added. Add the remaining butter, a piece at a time, stirring constantly until melted. Continue to cook and stir for 2 to 2½ minutes more or until sauce thickens. Immediately remove from heat. If sauce is too thick or curdles, immediately whisk in 1 to 2 tablespoons hot water. Season to taste with salt and pepper. Makes about 1½ cups.

The Machine Shed Farmer's Benedict Breakfast

Fruit Salad with Banana Dressing

Chai
Start to finish: 15 minutes

1¼ cups nonfat dry milk powder
¼   cup black tea leaves
1 or 2 cardamom pods
4   2-inch pieces stick cinnamon
2   teaspoons dried lemon peel

1. In two clean cellophane bags or two 6-ounce jars or bottles, layer all ingredients, dividing evenly. Seal bags or cover jars and store in a cool, dry place for up to 3 months.

2. To serve, in a large saucepan combine contents of bag with the water. Bring to boiling; remove from heat. Cover and let stand for 5 minutes. Strain through a wire sieve lined with 100% cotton cheesecloth or clean paper coffee filter.

3. To serve, add honey to sweeten to taste. Makes enough mix for 8, 1-cup servings.

Nutrition facts per serving: *40 calories, 0 g total fat, 0 g saturated fat, 2 mg cholesterol, 62 mg sodium, 6 g carbohydrate, 0 g fiber, 4 g protein, 5% DV Vitamin A, 2% DV Vitamin C, 13% DV calcium.*

Fruit Salad with Banana Dressing
Start to finish: 20 minutes

8   cups cut-up fruit, such as papaya, banana, strawberries, carambola (star fruit), cantaloupe, honeydew, mango, kiwi fruit, and/or blueberries
¼   cup toasted chopped walnuts
2   medium bananas, peeled and sliced
1   8-ounce carton lemon low-fat yogurt
2   tablespoons sugar
2   teaspoons lemon juice
    Lettuce leaves

For dressing, in a blender container combine sliced bananas, lemon yogurt, sugar, and lemon juice; cover and blend for 15 to 20 seconds or until smooth. Chill dressing, covered, for up to 2 hours. To serve, line salad plates with lettuce; arrange fruit on top. Top with dressing. Sprinkle with walnuts. Makes 8 side-dish servings.

Nutrition facts per serving: *202 calories, 3 g total fat, 0 g saturated fat, 1 mg cholesterol, 26 mg sodium, 41 g carbohydrate, 5 g fiber, 4 g protein, 21% DV Vitamin A, 124% DV Vitamin C, 6% DV calcium, 4% DV iron.*

Chai

Beef Hash with a Spicy Kick

Special start

When your family smells this sweet and spicy breakfast cooking, they'll have no trouble waking up. Rise and shine!

Beef Hash with a Spicy Kick

Prep: 30 minutes   Marinate: 30 minutes
Cook: 15 minutes

½ cup orange juice
2 tablespoons lime juice
1 tablespoon adobo sauce (from chipotle peppers)
1¼ pounds beef sirloin or top loin steak, finely chopped
2 large onions, diced (2 cups)
2 tablespoons minced garlic or bottled minced garlic
1 tablespoon chili powder
1 tablespoon cooking oil
1½ pound Yukon Gold potatoes or red skinned potatoes, cooked* and diced
1 tablespoon chopped chipotle peppers in adobo sauce
2 Roma tomatoes, seeded and hopped
¼ cup snipped fresh cilantro
   Salt and ground black pepper
   Fried eggs (optional)
   Fresh cilantro sprig (optional)

1. In a large plastic bag set in a bowl, combine orange juice, lime juice, and adobo sauce. Add meat, turning to coat. Close bag. Marinate in refrigerator for 30 minutes. Drain and discard marinade. Pat meat dry with clean white paper towels.

2. In a 12-inch heavy skillet cook the onion, garlic, and chili powder in hot oil over medium heat for 5 minutes or until onion is tender. Add meat to skillet; cook and stir about 2 minutes or until meat is browned. Stir in potatoes and chipotle peppers. Spread in an even layer in the skillet. Cook for 8 minutes more or until potatoes are golden brown, turning occasionally. Stir in tomatoes and snipped cilantro. Season with salt and pepper. Serve with fried eggs and fresh cilantro. Makes 6 servings.

*To Cook Potatoes: Remove eyes from potatoes. Cut potatoes into quarters. Cook, covered, in enough boiling lightly salted water to cover for 20 to 25 minutes or until tender. Drain.

Nutrition facts per serving: 263 calories, 6 g total fat, 2 g saturated fat, 1 g monounsaturated fat, 0 g polyunsaturated fat, 45 mg cholesterol, 189 mg sodium, 28 g carbohydrate, 4 g total sugar, 4 g fiber, 24 g protein, 51% DV Vitamin C, 6% DV calcium, 23% DV iron.

Better Homes and Gardens
Test Kitchen

TEST KITCHEN TIP: REMOVE AS MUCH MOISTURE AS POSSIBLE FROM THE MEAT TO MAKE A CRISPY HASH.

Caramel Apple Breakfast Pudding

Better Homes and Gardens®

Test Kitchen

Caramel Apple Breakfast Pudding

Prep: 30 minutes   Freeze: 3-24 hours
Cook: 40 minutes

2	large tart apples (such as Jonathan or Granny Smith)
¾	teaspoon ground cinnamon
½	cup packed brown sugar
2	tablespoons light-colored corn syrup
2	tablespoons margarine or butter
¼	cup pecan pieces
3	beaten eggs
1¼	cups milk
1	teaspoon vanilla
¼	teaspoon ground nutmeg
10	½-inch-thick slices Italian or French bread

1. Peel, core, and slice apples (should have 2 cups). In a small saucepan combine apple slices and ¼ cup water. Bring to boiling; reduce heat. Cook, covered, over medium-low heat for 5 to 7 minutes or until apples are tender, stirring occasionally. Drain in a colander. Transfer apples to a small bowl. Gently stir cinnamon into cooked apples. Set aside.

2. In the same small saucepan combine brown sugar, light-colored corn syrup, and margarine or butter. Cook and stir over medium heat until mixture just comes to a boil. Remove from heat. Pour mixture into a 2-quart square baking dish. Sprinkle pecans over all.

3. In a medium mixing bowl combine the eggs, milk, vanilla, and nutmeg. Arrange a layer of half the bread slices in the baking dish atop the caramel mixture, trimming bread to fit. Spoon cooked apples evenly over bread layer. Arrange remaining bread slices on top. Carefully pour the egg mixture over bread, pressing the bread down gently to moisten the slices completely. Cover with plastic wrap and refrigerate for 3 to 24 hours.

4. At serving time, uncover and bake in a 325°F. oven for 40 to 45 minutes or until a knife comes out clean. Remove from oven; run a knife around edge to loosen. Let stand for 15 minutes. Carefully invert pudding onto a platter. (Spoon any remaining caramel mixture in dish over pudding.) Cut into triangles. Serve warm or cool. Makes 8 servings.

Nutrition facts per serving: *208 calories, 7 g total fat, 2 g saturated fat, 83 mg cholesterol, 168 mg sodium, 31 g carbohydrate, 0 g fiber, 5 g protein, 9% DV Vitamin A, 7% DV calcium, 8% DV iron.*

Breakfast Yogurt
Prep: 10 minutes   Chill: 30 minutes

1   6- to 8-ounce carton vanilla or other
     flavored yogurt
½   small apple, cored and diced (¼ cup)
1   tablespoon quick-cooking rolled oats
1   tablespoon raisin bran cereal
     Assorted fruit (optional)

In a small bowl combine yogurt, apple, rolled
oats, and raisin bran cereal. Cover and chill
for 30 minutes. Top with fruit if desired. Makes
1 serving.

Nutrition facts per serving: *234 calories, 3 g total fat, 2 g
saturated fat, 11 mg cholesterol, 143 mg sodium, 45 g carbohydrate, 3 g fiber, 9 g protein, 10% DV Vitamin C, 31% DV
calcium, 3% DV iron.*

**TEST KITCHEN TIP: TO MAKE
AHEAD, PREPARE AS DIRECTED
ABOVE. COVER AND CHILL UP TO
8 HOURS.**

Sparkling Fruit Juice
Start to finish: 10 minutes

3   cups apricot nectar, chilled
1   cup orange juice, chilled
½   cup grapefruit juice, chilled
2   tablespoons lemon juice
3   cups sparkling mineral water, chilled
     Ice cubes
     Blood orange slices (optional)

In a large pitcher, stir together the apricot
nectar, orange juice, grapefruit juice, and
lemon juice. Slowly stir in the mineral water.
Serve juice mixture over ice. If desired, garnish
with blood orange slices. Makes 8 (8-ounce)
servings.

Nutrition facts per serving: *71 calories, 0 g total fat, 0 g
saturated fat, 0 mg cholesterol, 8 mg sodium, 18 g carbohydrate,
1 g fiber, 1 g protein.*

Breakfast Yogurt

take it to the *field*

Everyone has to eat, but when it's time for planting, harvest, or branding, there just isn't time to drop everything and head back to the house for lunch. That's where the farm wife comes in.

Farmers and hired hands work up an appetite, so skinny sandwiches won't do. They need real food. The kind of food that will stick to their ribs and keep them going until dinner. It has to be transportable, easy to eat, and, of course, delicious. And on the farm, no meal is complete without dessert.

Maybe the lunches you pack wind up in the school lunchroom or an office cubicle rather than in the field, but city slickers and farm folk alike will enjoy the taste of home in each of these hearty meals.

Eat, enjoy and GET BACK TO WORK!

Tasty traditions

The Machine Shed Pan-Fried Buttermilk Chicken

The Machine Shed Pan-Fried Buttermilk Chicken

  2   cups milk
  2   cups buttermilk
3½   to 4 pounds meaty chicken pieces (breast halves, thighs, and drumsticks)
  ½   cup all-purpose flour
  ½   teaspoon salt
  ¼   teaspoon ground black pepper
  2   to 3 tablespoons cooking oil

1. Skin chicken, if desired. In a large plastic bag set in a deep bowl, combine the milk and buttermilk. Add chicken pieces to bag; close bag. Chill for 2 to 4 hours, turning bag occasionally. Remove chicken. Drain and discard buttermilk mixture.

2. In a shallow dish combine the flour, salt, and pepper. Dip chicken pieces in flour mixture to coat, shaking off excess.

3. In a very large skillet heat oil over medium heat. Add chicken, in batches if necessary. Cook, uncovered, until chicken is browned, turning occasionally to brown evenly. Transfer chicken to a 15×10×1-inch baking pan.

4. Bake, uncovered, in a 350°F. oven for 45 to 50 minutes or until chicken is done (170°F. for breasts, 180°F. for thighs and drumsticks).

Strawberry Jam
Serve this homemade jam with your favorite bread.
Start to finish: 40 minutes

  2   quarts fresh strawberries, hulled
  1   1¾-ounce package powdered pectin
  ½   teaspoon margarine or butter
  7   cups sugar

1. Crush 1 cup of berries in an 8-quart pot. Continue adding berries and crushing until you have 5 cups crushed berries. Stir in pectin and margarine. Heat on high, stirring constantly, until mixture comes to a full rolling boil. Add sugar all at once. Return to boiling; boil 1 minute, stirring constantly. Remove from heat; skim off foam.

2. Ladle at once into hot, sterilized half-pint canning jars, leaving a ¼-inch headspace. Wipe jar rims; adjust lids. Process in a boiling-water canner 5 minutes. Remove jars; cool. Makes 8 half-pints (111 one-tablespoon servings).

Nutrition facts per serving: *46 calories, 0 g total fat, 0 mg cholesterol, 1 mg sodium, 12 g carbohydrate, 0 g fiber, 0 g protein, 8% DV Vitamin C.*

Once the chicken is finished baking, hold it in a warming oven until the rest of the meal is ready. This makes the chicken tender.

If you're serving this chicken at the table rather than in the field, try it with The Machine Shed's Garlic Mashed Potatoes. You'll find the recipe in the "Dinner vs. Supper" section of this cookbook.

THE MACHINE SHED
A restaurant honoring the American farmer ®

New Potato Salad

New Potato Salad

Prep: 40 minutes   Chill: 6 to 24 hours

2   pounds tiny new potatoes
1   cup low-fat mayonnaise dressing or
      light salad dressing
2   stalks celery, chopped
1   large onion, chopped
⅓   cup chopped sweet or dill pickles
½   teaspoon salt
¼   teaspoon coarsely ground black pepper
2   hard-cooked eggs, chopped
1   to 2 tablespoons fat-free milk
      Coarsely ground black pepper
      (optional)

1. In a large saucepan, combine potatoes and enough water to cover potatoes. Bring to boiling; reduce heat. Cover and simmer for 15 to 20 minutes or just until tender. Drain well; cool potatoes. Cut potatoes into quarters.

2. In a large bowl, combine mayonnaise dressing, celery, onion, pickles, the ½ teaspoon salt, and the ¼ teaspoon pepper. Add the potatoes and egg, gently tossing to coat. Cover and chill for 6 to 24 hours.

3. To serve, stir enough of the milk into salad to reach desired consistency. Season to taste with additional pepper. Makes 16 servings.

Nutrition facts per serving: *86 calories, 3 g total fat, 1 g saturated fat, 27 mg cholesterol, 254 mg sodium, 14 g carbohydrate, 1 g fiber, 2 g protein.*

Chocolate Chip Cookie Sticks

Prep: 35 minutes   Bake: 28 minutes
Cool: 1 hour   Stand: 1 hour

- ½   cup butter, softened
- ½   cup shortening
- 1   cup packed brown sugar
- ½   cup granulated sugar
- ½   teaspoon baking soda
- 2   eggs
- 2   teaspoons vanilla
- 2½ cups all-purpose flour
- 8   ounces coarsely chopped semisweet chocolate
- 1   cup chopped walnuts, pecans, hazelnuts (filberts) (optional)

1. Line a 13×9×2-inch baking pan with foil; set aside. In a large mixing bowl beat butter and shortening with an electric mixer on medium to high speed for 30 seconds. Add brown sugar, granulated sugar, and baking soda; beat until combined, scraping sides of bowl occassionally. Beat in the eggs and vanilla until combined. Beat in as much of the flour as you can with the mixer. Using a wooden spoon, stir in any remaining flour. Stir in chocolate and, if desired, nuts. Press dough evenly into the prepared pan.

2. Bake in a 375°F. oven for 22 to 25 minutes or until golden brown and center is set. Cool in pan on a wire rack 1 hour.

3. Preheat oven to 325°F. Holding securely to foil lining, gently remove cookies from pan and place on a cutting board, leaving cookies on foil lining. Cut crosswise into 9×½-inch slices. Place slices, cut side down, about 1 inch apart on an ungreased cookie sheet. Bake for 6 to 8 minutes or until cut edges are crispy. Carefully transfer cookies to wire rack (cookies will be tender). Cool. Makes 18.

Nutrition facts per serving: 333 calories, 20 g total fat, saturated fat, 37 mg cholesterol, 98 mg sodium, 39 g carbohydrate, 2 g fiber, 4 g protein.

Chocolate Chip Cookie Sticks

Better Homes and Gardens

Test Kitchen

TEST KITCHEN TIP: TO MAKE AHEAD, BAKE COOKIES AS DIRECTED; COOL COMPLETELY. PLACE IN A FREEZER CONTAINER OR BAG AND FREEZE FOR UP TO 3 MONTHS. BEFORE SERVING, THAW FOR 15 MINUTES.

No utensils needed

This delicious lunch combines hot and spicy with cool and refreshing.
Serve the spiky cucumber salad in a cup, and it's instant finger-food!

Pulled Pork Sandwiches with Root Beer Sauce

Pulled Pork Sandwiches with Root Beer Sauce

Prep: 25 minutes   Cook: 4 hours

1	2½- to 3-pound pork sirloin roast
½	teaspoon pepper
1	tablespoon cooking oil
2	medium onions, cut into thin wedges
1	cup root beer
2	tablespoons minced garlic
3	cups root beer (two 12-oz. cans or bottles)
1	cup bottled chili sauce
¼	teaspoon root beer concentrate (optional)
6	to 8 dashes hot pepper sauce (optional)
8	to 10 hamburger buns, split (and toasted, if desired)
	Lettuce leaves (optional)
	Tomato slices (optional)

1. Trim fat from meat. If necessary, cut roast to fit into crockery cooker. Sprinkle meat with the salt and pepper. In a large skillet brown roast on all sides in hot oil. Drain. Transfer meat to a 3½-, 4-, or 5-quart electric crockery cooker. Add onions, the 1 cup root beer, and garlic. Cover; cook on low-heat setting for 8 to 10 hours or on high-heat setting for 4 to 5 hours.

2. Meanwhile, for sauce, in a medium saucepan combine the 2 cans or bottles of root beer and bottled chili sauce. Bring to boiling; reduce heat.

3. Boil gently, uncovered, stirring occasionally, about 30 minutes or until mixture is reduced to 2 cups. Add root beer concentrate and bottled hot pepper sauce, if desired.

4. Transfer roast to a cutting board or serving platter. With a slotted spoon, remove onions from juices and place on serving platter. Discard juices. Using two forks, pull meat apart into shreds. To serve, line buns with lettuce leaves and tomato slices, if desired. Add meat and onions; spoon on sauce. Makes 8 to 10 servings.

Nutrition facts per serving: *356 calories, 10 g fat, 3 g saturated fat, 59 mg cholesterol, 786 mg sodium, 44 g carbohydrate, 1 g fiber, 22 g protein, 4% DV Vitamin A, 9% DV Vitamin C, 4% DV calcium, 13% DV iron.*

TEST KITCHEN TIP: TO MAKE AHEAD, TRANSFER PORK MIXTURE TO COVERED CONTAINER AND CHILL UP TO 24 HOURS. OR TRANSFER TO 1-, 2-, OR 4-SERVING FREEZER CONTAINERS; SEAL, LABEL, AND FREEZE UP TO 1 MONTH. THAW OVERNIGHT BEFORE SERVING. TO REHEAT, TRANSFER TO SAUCEPAN; COVER AND HEAT OVER MEDIUM-LOW HEAT UNTIL HEATED THROUGH, STIRRING OCCASIONALLY. IF NECESSARY, ADD 2 TO 4 TABLESPOONS WATER TO KEEP MIXTURE FROM STICKING.

Better Homes and Gardens

Test Kitchen

take it to the
field

Roasted Tomato Salsa

Prep: 20 minutes   Chill: 4 hours
Roast: 25 minutes   Cool: 20 minutes
Stand: 20 minutes

2½	pounds roma tomatoes (about 15)
3	fresh jalapeño peppers
1	medium head garlic
1	teaspoon salt
2	medium white onions, finely chopped
⅔	cup lightly packed cilantro leaves, snipped (¼ cup)
4	teaspoons cider vinegar
	Tortilla chips

1. Core the tomatoes. Place in one side of a 15×10×1-inch baking pan. Halve the jalapeño peppers. Remove stems and seeds. Place, cut side down, in the other side of baking pan with tomatoes. Peel away outer skin from garlic. Cut off the pointed top portion with a knife, leaving the bulb intact but exposing the individual cloves. Add to pan. Roast, uncovered, in a 450°F. oven for 25 minutes or until tomatoes are soft and pepper skins are charred. Cool.

2. Remove tomato skins. Press to remove garlic paste from individual cloves of garlic. Place garlic, jalapeno peppers, and salt in a food processor bowl or blender container. Cover and process or blend with a few pulses until finely chopped. Add half of the tomatoes; cover and process or blend with a few pulses until coarsely chopped. Transfer to a large mixing bowl. Add remaining tomatoes to food processor bowl or blender container; cover and process or blend with a few pulses until coarsely chopped. Stir into tomato mixture in bowl.

3. Stir onions, cilantro, and vinegar into tomato mixture until combined. Cover and chill several hours to blend flavors. Serve with tortilla chips. Makes about 4 cups.

Nutrition facts per serving: *24 calories, 0 g total fat, 0 g saturated fat, 0 mg cholesterol, 154 mg sodium, 5 g carbohdrate, 1 g fiber, 1 g protein, 29% DV Vitamin C, 1% DV calcium, 3% DV iron.*

Roasted Tomato Salsa

Spiky Cucumber Salad

Prep: 20 minutes   Chill: 2 hours

- ½   cup rice vinegar
- ¼   cup olive oil
- 1   tablespoon finely shredded lemon peel
- 2   tablespoons lemon juice
- 1   tablespoon grated fresh ginger
- 1   tablespoon sugar
- 1½   teaspoons coarsely ground black pepper
- 1   teaspoon toasted sesame oil
- 1   teaspoon salt
- ¼   teaspoon crushed red pepper
- 8   medium cucumbers

1. In a screw-top jar combine vinegar, olive oil, lemon peel and juice, ginger, sugar, black pepper, sesame oil, salt, and crushed red pepper. Close jar; shake well to combine. Set aside.

2. Cut cucumbers into bite-sized strips or sticks. Place cucumbers in a very large bowl. Drizzle dressing over cucumbers; toss to combine. Cover and refrigerate for at least 2 hours or up to 12 hours, tossing occasionally. Drain to serve. Makes 24 to 26 servings.

Nutrition facts per serving: *27 calories, 1 g total fat, 0 g saturated fat, 1 g monounsaturated fat, 0 g polyunsaturated fat, 0 mg cholesterol, 51 mg sodium, 3 g carbohydrate, 3 g total sugar, 1 g fiber, 1 g protein, 10% DV Vitamin C, 2% DV calcium, 2% DV iron.*

One-Handed Fried Pies

One-Handed Fried Pies

Prep: 35 minutes   Cook: 36 minutes

- 1½   cups dried peaches, apricots, and/or apples (6 ounces)
- 1¼   cups apple cider
- 2   cups all-purpose flour
- 2   teaspoons baking powder
- 2   teaspoons granulated sugar
- ¼   teaspoon salt
- ¼   teaspoon baking soda
- ½   cup shortening
- ⅔   cup buttermilk or ⅓ cup buttermilk and ⅓ cup whipping cream
        Water
- 4   tablespoons shortening
        Sifted powdered sugar

1. For the filling, in a saucepan combine dried fruit and apple cider. Bring to boiling; reduce heat. Simmer, covered for 20 to 25 minutes or until fruit is tender (cider should be cooked down). Mash slightly. Cool.

2. Meanwhile, for the pastry, in a bowl combine flour, baking powder, sugar, salt, and baking soda. Using a pastry blender, cut in the ½ cup shortening until pieces are pea-size.

3. Sprinkle 1 tablespoon of the buttermilk or buttermilk mixture over part of the flour mixture; gently toss with a fork. Push moistened dough to the side. Repeat, using 1 tablespoon of the buttermilk at a time, until all the dough is moistened. If pastry seems dry, add a little water, 1 tablespoon at a time. (Do not overhandle.) Form dough into ball.

4. Pat or lightly roll dough into a 15-inch circle. Using a 4-inch round cutter, cut the dough into 12 circles, rerolling dough as needed. Place about 1 tablespoon fruit on half of each circle. Moisten edges of circles with water. Fold over into half-moon shape. Seal edges with tines of a fork.

5. In a 12-inch nonstick skillet heat 2 tablespoons of the shortening over medium-low heat. Fry half of the pies for 8 to 10 minutes or until golden brown, turning once. Drain on paper towels. (Add remaining shortening; fry remaining pies.) Serve warm.

Chocolate Fried Pies: Omit fruit filling. Prepare pastry as directed. For chocolate filling, in a small bowl combine ½ cup sifted powdered sugar and ¼ cup unsweetened cocoa powder. Stir in 4 tablespoons melted butter. Spread a scant 2 teaspoons of mixture onto each pastry circle. Fry pies as directed.

Nutrition facts per serving: *258 calories, 13 g total fat, 3 g saturated fat, 0 mg cholesterol, 158 mg sodium, 34 g carbohydrate, 2 g fiber, 3 g protein, 7% DV Vitamin A, 3% DV Vitamin C, 8% DV calcium, 11% DV iron.*

Spiky Cucumber Salad

take it to the *field*
lamb for lunch

This savory meal is just right for cool days. Use fresh vegetables from your garden or the farmer's market for dipping.

Grilled Lambburger Roll-Ups
Prep: 15 minutes   Grill: 14 minutes

1	beaten egg
3	tablespoons fine dry bread crumbs
2	tablespoons snipped fresh oregano
2	cloves garlic, minced
¾	teaspoon salt
½	teaspoon freshly ground pepper
1	pound lean ground lamb
2	14- to 15-inch soft cracker bread rounds or four 7- to 8-inch flour tortillas
⅓	cup prepared hummus (garbanzo bean spread)
4	cups torn spinach or red-tipped leaf lettuce
¼	cup crumbled feta cheese
3	tablespoons sliced pitted kalamata or ripe olives

1. In a large bowl combine egg, bread crumbs, oregano, garlic, salt, pepper, and 1 tablespoon water. Add lamb; mix well. Form into eight 4-inch-long logs.

2. Grill lamb on the rack of an uncovered grill directly over medium coals for 14 to 18 minutes or until lamb is no longer pink, turning once. (Or, place in shallow baking pan. Bake in a 400°F. oven for 12 to 14 minutes.)

3. Meanwhile, spread the cracker bread or tortillas with hummus. Sprinkle with spinach or lettuce, feta cheese, and olives. If using cracker bread, place 4 lamb pieces, end to end, near an edge of each round. Roll up, beginning with edge closest to lamb. Slice each roll-up diagonally in fourths. (If using tortillas, place 2 lamb pieces, end to end, on each tortilla. Roll up. Slice each roll-up diagonally in half.) Makes 4 servings.

Nutrition facts per serving: 625 calories, 26 g total fat, 9 g saturated fat, 135 mg cholesterol, 1225 mg sodium, 64 g carbohydrate, 2 g fiber, 34 g protein, 41% DV Vitamin A, 30% DV Vitamin C, 11% DV calcium, 38% DV iron.

Grilled Lamburger Roll-Ups

Mixed Citrus Salad

Start to finish: 20 minutes

2	pink or red grapefruit
2	navel oranges
½	cup salad oil
1	teaspoon finely shredded lemon peel
¼	cup lemon juice
2	teaspoons sugar
1	tablespoon Dijon-style mustard
¼	teaspoon pepper
4	cups thinly sliced Belgian endive
4	cups torn escarole
1	small jicama, peeled and cut into matchsticks (about 2 cups)

1. Peel and section grapefruit and oranges over a bowl; reserve any juices.

2. For dressing, in a screw-top jar combine reserved fruit juices, salad oil, lemon peel, lemon juice, sugar, mustard, and pepper. Cover; shake well.

3. Place greens on a large serving plate. Arrange fruit and jicama atop greens. Drizzle dressing over top. Serve immediately. Makes 10 side-dish servings.

Nutrition facts per serving: *143 calories, 11 g total fat, 2 g saturated fat, 0 mg cholesterol, 42 mg sodium, 11 g carbohydrate, 2 g fiber, 1 g protein, 6% DV Vitamin A, 62% DV Vitamin C, 2% DV calcium, 3% DV iron.*

Mixed Citrus Salad

Carrot Dip with Vegetable Spears

Carrot Dip with Vegetable Spears

Prep: 20 minutes   Chill: Overnight

½ of an 8-ounce carton dairy sour cream
½ of an 8-ounce package cream cheese, softened
¼ cup mayonnaise or salad dressing
2 teaspoons soy sauce
1½ teaspoons prepared horseradish (optional)
¼ teaspoon salt
¼ teaspoon ground black pepper
1½ cups finely shredded carrots
⅓ cup chopped green onions
   Dippers such as flatbreads, crackers, tortilla chips, celery sticks, sweet pepper strips, jicama sticks, and/or zucchini sticks

1. In a medium mixing bowl beat together sour cream, cream cheese, mayonnaise, soy sauce, horseradish (if using), salt, and pepper with an electric mixer until smooth. Stir in shredded carrots and green onions until combined.

2. Cover and chill for 4 to 24 hours (do not prepare further ahead than this or the dip will become too thin). Keep the dip chilled while transporting. Stir dip before serving with dippers. Makes 2 cups (about 10 servings).

Nutrition facts per serving: *110 calories, 10 g fat, 4 g saturated fat, 2 g monounsaturated fat, 3 g polyunsaturated fat, 19 mg cholesterol, 195 mg sodium, 3 g carbohydrate, 2 g total sugar, 1 g fiber, 2 g protein, 4% DV Vitamin C, 3% DV Calcium, 2% DV iron.*

Pumpkin Bars
Prep: 20 minutes   Bake: 25 minutes

2   cups all-purpose flour
2   teaspoons baking powder
2   teaspoons ground cinnamon
1   teaspoon baking soda
¼   teaspoon salt
4   eggs
1   15-ounce can pumpkin
1⅔ cups sugar
1   cup cooking oil
¾   cup chopped pecans (optional)
1   recipe Cream Cheese Frosting (see recipe below)
    Pecan halves (optional)

1. In a medium bowl stir together flour, baking powder, cinnamon, baking soda, and salt; set aside. In a large mixing bowl beat together eggs, pumpkin, sugar, and oil. Add the flour mixture; beat until well combined. Stir in chopped pecans, if desired.

2. Spread batter in an ungreased 15×10×1-inch baking pan. Bake in a 350°F. oven for 25 to 30 minutes or until toothpick inserted in center comes out clean. Cool on wire rack. Frost with Cream Cheese Frosting. Top with pecan halves, if desired. Cut into squares. Store in refrigerator. Makes 24 bars.

Cream Cheese Frosting: In a medium bowl beat together one 3-ounce package cream cheese, softened; ¼ cup butter or margarine, softened; and 1 teaspoon vanilla until fluffy. Gradually add 2 cups sifted powdered sugar, beating until smooth.

Nutrition facts per serving: *250 calories, 13 g total fat, 4 g saturated fat, 4 mg cholesterol, 147 mg sodium, 31 g carbohydrate, 1 g fiber, 3 g protein, 43% DV Vitamin A, 1% DV Vitamin C, 3% DV calcium, 6% DV iron.*

Pumpkin Bars

WISCONSIN CHEESE

CHICKEN NOODLE

TOMATO BASIL

perfect pockets

Pour the tomato sipper into an insulated travel cup, and your farmhands can enjoy it from the driver's seat of the tractor or combine (or SUV or minivan).

Pork Tenderloin in Cornbread

Prep: 25 minutes   Roast: 35 minutes

- 1¼ cups all-purpose flour
- ¼ cup cornmeal
- 1 teaspoon sugar
- ¾ teaspoon baking powder
- ¼ cup cooking oil
- 1 beaten egg
- 3 tablespoons water
- 2 to 3 tablespoons snipped fresh cilantro or parsley
- 1 teaspoon chili powder
- ¼ teaspoon salt
- ¼ teaspoon pepper
- 1 12- to 14-ounce pork tenderloin
- ¾ cup salsa or picante sauce
- ¼ teaspoon salt
- Lemon leaves (optional)

Pork Tenderloin in Cornbread

1. Mix the flour, cornmeal, sugar, baking powder, and ¼ teaspoon salt. Combine oil, egg, and water. Stir liquid mixture into dry mixture until well blended, forming a ball.

2. On a lightly floured piece of waxed paper, roll or pat the dough into an 8-inch square. Combine the cilantro, chili powder, ¼ teaspoon salt, and pepper. Rub cilantro mixture on surface of pork, coating evenly. Place tenderloin across center of dough, folding under narrow end of tenderloin to make an even thickness. With the aid of the waxed paper, roll dough around tenderloin. Seal edge and ends. Place seam side down on a lightly greased baking sheet.

3. Roast in a 425°F. oven 20 minutes. Cover loosely with foil; roast 15 to 20 minutes more or until a meat thermometer inserted in center of meat registers 155°F. Let stand 5 minutes. Serve with salsa. If desired, garnish with lemon leaves. Makes 4 servings.

Nutrition facts per serving: *434 calories, 19 g total fat, 3 g saturated fat, 104 mg cholesterol, 674 mg sodium, 42 g carbohydrate, 25 g protein.*

take it to the
field

Spicy Hot Tomato Sipper

Strawberry Spinach Toss
Start to finish: 25 minutes

5	cups torn spinach
1	cup sliced strawberries
1	cup honeydew melon or cantaloupe balls
2	ounces Gouda or Edam cheese, cut into thin bite-size strips
⅓	cup coarsely chopped pecans, toasted
2	tablespoons lime juice
2	tablespoons honey
1	tablespoons salad oil
½	teaspoon fresh ginger or ¼ tsp. ground ginger

In a salad bowl, toss together spinach, strawberries, melon, cheese, and pecans. For dressing, in a screw-top jar, combine remaining ingredients. Cover; shake well. Pour some dressing over spinach mixture. Toss to coat. Pass remaining dressing. Makes 6 side-dish servings.

Nutrition facts per serving: *145 calories, 9 g fat, 2 g saturated fat, 11 mg cholesterol, 119 mg sodium, 13 g carbohydrate, 2 g fiber, 4 g protein.*

Spicy Hot Tomato Sipper
Start to finish: 15 minutes

1¼	teaspoons ground cumin
1	46-ounce can tomato juice
⅓	cup lime juice
¼	teaspoon ground black pepper
⅛	teaspoon ground red pepper
	Fresh cilantro sprigs (optional)
	Lime peel curls (optional)

1. Heat a large saucepan over low heat for 1 to 2 minutes or until hot. Place cumin in saucepan. Cook and stir over low heat for 30 seconds. Carefully add tomato juice, lime juice, black pepper, and red pepper. Bring mixture to boiling, stirring occasionally; remove from heat. Serve immediately. (Or, cool; cover and store in the refrigerator for up to 3 days. To reheat, place mixture in a large saucepan. Heat over high heat until hot, stirring occasionally.)

2. To serve, ladle into mugs. If desired, top each with cilantro sprig and lime peel curl. Makes 16 (6-ounce) servings.

Nutrition facts per serving: *17 calories, 0 g total fat, 0 g saturated fat, 0 mg cholesterol, 294 mg sodium, 4 g carbohydrate, 1 g fiber, 1 g protein, 4% DV Vitamin A, 13% DV Vitamin C, 4% DV iron.*

TEST KITCHEN TIP: UP TO 3 DAYS AHEAD, PREPARE THE SIPPER; COVER AND CHILL. TO SERVE, REHEAT AS DIRECTED.

Better Homes and Gardens
Test Kitchen

Strawberry Spinach Toss

Delicious Lemon Cupcakes
Prep: 20 minutes   Bake: 18 minutes

3½   cups all-purpose flour
 2   teaspoons baking powder
 1   teaspoon baking soda
 ½   teaspoon salt
 1   cup butter, softened
1½   cups granulated sugar
 2   teaspoons vanilla
 3   eggs
 2   8-ounce cartons dairy sour cream
 2   teaspoons finely shredded lemon peel
 3   tablespoons butter, softened
 1   cup sifted powdered sugar
 2   tablespoons lemon juice
 ¾   teaspoon vanilla
1¼   cups sifted powdered sugar
     Milk (2 to 3 teaspoons if necessary)
 1   teaspoon shredded lemon peel

1. Preheat the oven to 350°F. Line thirty 2½-inch muffin cups with paper bake cups; set aside. In a medium bowl, combine flour, baking powder, baking soda, and salt; set aside.

2. In a large bowl, beat butter with an electric mixer on medium to high speed for 30 seconds. Add granulated sugar and vanilla; beat until well mixed. Add eggs, one at a time, beating well after each addition. Add flour mixture and sour cream alternately to beaten mixture, beating on low speed after each addition just until combined. (The batter will be thick.) Stir in lemon peel.

3. Spoon about ¼ cup of the batter into each prepared muffin cup. Bake in the preheated oven about 18 minutes or until a wooden toothpick inserted in centers comes out clean. Cool completely on a wire rack. Makes 30 cupcakes.

Lemon Frosting: In a medium bowl, beat 3 tablespoons butter, softened, until fluffy. Gradually add 1 cup sifted powdered sugar, beating well. Gradually beat in 2 tablespoons lemon juice and ¾ teaspoon vanilla. Gradually beat in 1¼ cups sifted powdered sugar. If necessary, beat in enough additional milk (2 to 3 teaspoons) to make spreading consistency. Stir in 1 teaspoon finely shredded lemon peel.

Nutrition facts per serving: *229 calories, 12 g total fat, 7 g saturated fat, 49 mg cholesterol, 201 mg sodium, 29 g carbohydrate, 0 g fiber, 3 g protein.0 g fiber, 4 g protein, 5% DV Vitamin A, 2% DV Vitamin C, 13% DV calcium.*

Better Homes and Gardens Test Kitchen

TEST KITCHEN TIP: IF ALL OF THE CUPCAKES DO NOT FIT IN THE OVEN AT ONE TIME, REFRIGERATE THE REMAINING CUPCAKES WHILE THE FIRST ONES BAKE.

Delicious Lemon Cupcakes

Jalapeño Steak Sandwiches

Grilling greats

Except for the muffins, this entire meal can be prepared on the grill, which means great taste and no mess in the kitchen. Fire up the grill, then feed those farmhands!

Jalapeño Steak Sandwiches

Prep: 25 minutes   Marinate: 4 hours
Cook: 14 minutes

6	cloves garlic, minced
3	jalapeño peppers, finely chopped (don't seed)
⅓	cup olive oil
⅓	cup fresh lime juice
3	tablespoons Dijon-style mustard
1	teaspoon kosher salt or salt
1¼	to 1½ pounds beef flank steak
12	slices Texas toast or other thick-cut white bread, toasted
½	cup purchased chipotle mayonnaise or ½ cup mayonnaise with 1 teaspoon chili powder
1	red onion, quartered and thinly sliced
4	ounces queso fresco or farmer cheese, crumbled
	Fresh cilantro sprigs
	Lime wedges

1. For marinade, in a bowl whisk together garlic, jalapeño peppers, olive oil, lime juice, mustard, and salt.

2. Trim fat from meat. With a sharp knife score meat on both sides at 1-inch intervals in diamond pattern. Place meat in a self-sealing plastic bag set in a shallow dish. Pour marinade over meat; seal bag. Marinate in refrigerator for 4 to 24 hours.

3. Heat a nonstick or well-seasoned grill pan on stovetop over medium heat. Drain meat; discard marinade. Place meat in hot pan. Cook for 14 to 16 minutes or until steak is medium, turning once halfway through grilling. Carve steak diagonally across the grain into thin slices.

4. Meanwhile, spread one side of each toast slice with mayonnaise. Place steak, onions, cheese, and cilantro on half the toast slices. Top with remaining slices. Serve with lime wedges. Makes 6 servings.

For tabletop grill: Preheat grill according to manufacturer's directions. Place steak on grill rack. If using a covered grill, close lid. Grill until steak is desired doneness. For covered grill, allow 7 to 9 minutes. (For open grill, allow 12 to 14 minutes for medium, turning once halfway through grilling.) Thinly slice steak diagonally across the grain. Continue as directed in Step 4 above.

Nutrition facts per serving: *560 calories, 28 g total fat, 6 g saturated fat, 8 g monounsaturated fat, 1 g polyunsaturated fat, 158 mg cholesterol, 965 mg sodium, 46 mg carbohydrate, 9 g total sugar, 0 g fiber, 36 g protein, 9% DV Vitamin C, 15% DV calcium, 26% DV iron.*

Better Homes and Gardens Test Kitchen

TEST KITCHEN TIP: TO TOAST BREAD IN A GRILL PAN OR AN OPEN GRILL, PLACE ON GRILL RACK AND ALLOW 1 TO 2 MINUTES PER SIDE. (INSTEAD OF A COVERED GRILL, USE A TOASTER.)

Grilled Vegetable Salad

Grilled Vegetable Salad

Prep: 20 minutes   Grill: 8 minutes

1   **medium red onion, cut into**
    ¾-inch-thick slices
1   **medium eggplant, cut crosswise**
    into 1-inch-thick slices
2   **large red sweet peppers, cut into**
    ¾-inch-thick rings
6   **thin asparagus spears, trimmed**
1   **medium zucchini, sliced lengthwise**
    into ¼-inch slices
1   **medium yellow squash, sliced**
    lengthwise into ¼-inch slices
¼   **cup olive oil**
6   **cups torn mixed greens**
¼   **cup snipped fresh basil**
¼   **cup balsamic vinegar**

1. Brush vegetables with olive oil and, if desired, sprinkle each side with freshly ground pepper and salt. Lay vegetables perpendicular to wires on rack of an uncovered grill directly over medium to medium-hot coals. Grill onion, eggplant, and pepper rings for 8 to 10 minutes. Grill asparagus, zucchini, and yellow squash for 5 to 6 minutes or until crisp-tender, turning occasionally.

2. Arrange vegetables on mixed greens. Drizzle with vinegar and sprinkle with basil. Makes 6 side-dish servings.

Nutrition facts per serving: *139 calories, 9 g total fat, 1 g saturated fat, 0 mg cholesterol, 24 mg sodium, 13 g carbohydrate, 4 g fiber, 3 g protein, 38% DV Vitamin A, 101% DV Vitamin C, 3% DV calcium, 11% DV iron.*

Better Homes and Gardens® Test Kitchen

TEST KITCHEN TIP: TO USE AN INDOOR GRILL: PREHEAT INDOOR ELECTRIC GRILL. BRUSH VEGETABLES WITH OLIVE OIL AND, IF DESIRED, SPRINKLE WITH SALT AND FRESHLY GROUND BLACK PEPPER. PLACE VEGETABLES ON THE GRILL RACK. (IF NECESSARY, COOK VEGETABLES IN BATCHES.) IF USING A COVERED GRILL, CLOSE LID. GRILL UNTIL VEGETABLES ARE CRISP-TENDER. (FOR A COVERED GRILL, ALLOW 4 TO 5 MINUTES. FOR AN UNCOVERED GRILL, ALLOW 8 TO 10 MINUTES FOR EGGPLANT, SWEET PEPPERS, AND ONION, AND 5 TO 6 MINUTES FOR ASPARAGUS, ZUCCHINI, AND YELLOW SQUASH, TURNING OCCASIONALLY TO COOK EVENLY.) SERVE AS ABOVE.

Grillside Potato Chips
Prep: 10 minutes   Grill: 15 minutes

1 pound potatoes (russet or long white), cut diagonally into 1/16-inch slices
3 tablespoons cooking oil
½ teaspoon dried thyme, crushed
½ teaspoon coarse salt or seasoned salt

1. Place potato slices in a Dutch oven. Add enought water to cover. Bring just to boiling. Cook for 2 to 3 minutes or until potatoes are crisp-tender; drain. Place in a single layer on paper towels. Carefully brush both sides of potato slices with cooking oil. Sprinkle with thyme and salt.

2. Preheat gas grill. Reduce heat to medium-high. Place potato slices on the grill rack directly over heat. Cover and grill for 15 to 20 minutes or until potatoes are browned, turning occasionally. Remove from grill. Let stand on a paper-towel-lined baking sheet for 8 to 10 minutes. (Chips will crisp as they stand.) Makes 4 servings.

Nutrition facts per serving: *209 calories, 10 g total fat, 1 g saturated fat, 0 mg cholesterol, 276 mg sodium, 27 g carbohydrate, 1 g fiber, 3 g protein, 28% DV Vitamin C, 1% DV calcium, 9% DV iron.*

TEST KITCHEN TIP: TO USE A CHARCOAL GRILL, GRILL SEASONED, PRECOOKED POTATOES ON GRILL RACK OVER MEDIUM COALS FOR 15 TO 20 MINUTES, TURNING OCCASIONALLY. SERVE AS ABOVE.

Grillside Potato Chips

Chocolate Cheesecake Muffins
Prep: 20 minutes   Bake: 20 minutes

1 3-ounce package cream cheese, softened
2 tablespoons granulated sugar
1 egg yolk
1½ cups all-purpose flour
½ cup granulated sugar
¼ cup unsweetened cocoa powder
2 teaspoons baking powder
¼ teaspoon salt
1 egg
¾ cup milk
¼ cup cooking oil
½ cup chopped walnuts
2 teaspoons powdered sugar

1. Grease twelve 2½-inch muffin cups or line them with paper bake cups.

2. Beat cream cheese, the 2 tablespoons sugar, and the egg yolk in a small mixing bowl with an electric mixer on medium speed until blended. Set aside.

3. Stir together flour, the ½ cup sugar, cocoa powder, baking powder, and salt in a medium mixing bowl. Make a well in the center of the dry ingredients; set aside.

4. Combine the whole egg, milk, and oil in another medium mixing bowl. Add egg mixture all at once to dry ingredients. Stir just until moistened (batter should be lumpy). Fold in walnuts.

5. Spoon half of the batter into prepared muffin cups (about 1 tablespoon in each muffin cup). Spoon about 1½ teaspoons cream cheese mixture on top of the batter in each cup. Spoon remaining batter into muffin cups, filling each cup two-thirds full.

6. Bake in a 400°F. oven about 20 minutes or until tops are dry. Cool in muffin cups on a wire rack for 5 minutes. Remove muffins from muffin cups. Sift powdered sugar over top of each muffin. Serve warm or cool. Cover and store any leftovers in the refrigerator up to 3 days. Makes 12 muffins.

TEST KITCHEN TIP: TO MAKE AHEAD, BAKE MUFFINS AS DIRECTED; COOL COMPLETELY. PLACE MUFFINS IN A FREEZER CONTAINER OR BAG, AND FREEZE UP TO 3 MONTHS. TO SERVE, WRAP THE FROZEN MUFFINS IN FOIL; BAKE IN A 300°F. OVEN FOR 15 TO 18 MINUTES OR UNTIL WARM.

dinner vs supper

It's a question that's been around as long as apron-clad wives and mothers have been serving meatloaf, scalloped potatoes and green beans. What do you call the evening meal – dinner or supper?

Your choice of wording may be due in part to where you live. In certain parts of the country, if you ask someone to come for dinner, they'll ring your doorbell around Noon. In other places, look for them around 5:00. But it's not always that simple, and sometimes people in the same family can't even agree on what to call the meal.

According to *The Columbia Guide to Standard American English*, dinner is the main meal of the day, whether served at Noon or in the evening. Supper is the evening meal, especially if dinner is the midday meal.

Whatever you choose to call these hearty meals, they're delicious, and the whole family will come running when you ring the dinner bell.

Or is it the supper bell?

southern comfort

Even if you live north of the Mason-Dixon line, you can still enjoy the great taste of the South.

Cajun-Flavored Catfish

Cajun-Flavored Catfish

Prep: 10 minutes   Bake: 15 minutes

1	tablespoon black pepper
1	tablespoon dried oregano, crushed
2	to 3 teaspoons seasoned salt
2	teaspoons onion powder
1	teaspoon crushed red pepper
¾	teaspoon chili powder
½	teaspoon ground cumin
4	skinned catfish fillets (about ½ inch thick)

1. Preheat oven to 350°F. In a small bowl stir together black pepper, oregano, salt, onion powder, crushed red pepper, chili powder, and ground cumin. Use about 1 tablespoon seasoning mixture to coat both sides of catfish. Arrange fish in lightly greased shallow baking pan.

2. Bake for 10 minutes. Turn fish over and continue baking for 5 to 8 minutes more or until fish just flakes easily when tested with a fork. Makes 4 servings.

Nutrition facts per serving: *223 calories, 13 g total fat, 79 mg cholesterol, 283 mg sodium, 1 g carbohydrate, 0 g fiber, 27 g protein, 3% DV Vitamin A, 2% DV Vitamin C, 2% DV calcium, 6% DV iron.*

Hush Puppies

Prep: 15 minutes   Cook: 30 minutes

1	egg
2½	cups buttermilk
¼	cup melted shortening, cooled slightly
1	tablespoon finely chopped onion
1¼	pounds (3¾ cups) self-rising cornmeal
¼	cup self-rising flour
1	tablespoon sugar
	Shortening or cooking oil for deep-fat frying

1. In a medium mixing bowl stir together eggs, buttermilk, the ¼ cup melted shortening, and onion. In another bowl combine cornmeal, flour, and sugar. Add egg mixture to cornmeal mixture and stir just until moistened.

2. Drop batter by tablespoons, 4 to 5 at a time, into deep hot fat (375°F.). Fry about 1 minute or until golden, turning once. Drain on paper towels. Keep cooked hush puppies warm on a baking sheet in a 300°F. oven while frying remaining dough. Makes about 55.

Nutrition facts per serving: *80 calories, 4 g total fat, 5 g cholesterol, 159 mg sodium, 9 g carbohydrate, 1 g fiber, 1 g protein, 5% DV calcium, 3% DV iron.*

TEST KITCHEN TIP: STORE REMAINING SEASONING MIX IN AN AIRTIGHT CONTAINER AT ROOM TEMPERATURE UP TO 1 MONTH. USE FOR FISH OR PORK.

The Machine Shed Coleslaw

The Machine Shed Coleslaw

12   cups shredded cabbage
      with carrot (coleslaw mix)
      (1½ 16-ounce packages)
 1   cup mayonnaise or salad
      dressing
 ½   cup sugar
 ½   teaspoon celery seeds

1. Place cabbage with carrot in a very large bowl; set aside.

2. In a medium bowl stir together mayonnaise, sugar, and celery seeds. Add to cabbage mixture and toss to coat.

3. Cover and chill up to 4 hours. Makes 8 servings.

THE MACHINE SHED
A restaurant honoring the American farmer ®

FARMER'S FAVORITE

Fried Green Tomatoes
Prep: 20 minutes   Cook: 4 minutes

1   pound green tomatoes
    (about 4 tomatoes)
½   cup white cornmeal
¼   cup all-purpose flour
2   tablespoons sesame seed
¼   teaspoon onion salt
⅛   teaspoon pepper
1   beaten egg
2   tablespoons milk
    Cooking oil for frying

1. Slice tomatoes into ¼-inch-thick slices. In a pie plate or baking dish combine cornmeal, flour, sesame seed, onion salt, and pepper. In a small mixing bowl combine egg and milk. Dip tomatoes slices into egg mixture, then coat both sides of tomato slices with the cornmeal mixture.

2. In a heavy large skillet heat about ¼ inch of cooking oil over medium heat. Fry tomato slices in a single layer about 2 minutes on each side or until golden brown. Drain on paper towels. Keep slices warm in a 300°F. oven while frying remaining tomatoes. Serve immediately. Makes 4 to 6 servings.

Nutrition facts per serving: *202 calories, 13 g total fat, 2 g saturated fat, 54 mg cholesterol, 136 mg sodium, 16 g carbohydrate, 6 g protein.*

Fried Green Tomatoes

Better Homes and Gardens®

Test Kitchen

TEST KITCHEN TIP: TO MAKE AHEAD, PREPARE AS DIRECTED THROUGH STEP 2. COVER AND CHILL IN AN AIRTIGHT CONTAINER FOR UP TO 24 HOURS.

Southern Black-Eyed Pea Salad

Southern Black-Eyed Pea Salad

Prep: 20 minutes   Chill: 4 to 24 hours

- 2 tablespoons cooking oil
- 4 small yellow summer squash, quartered lengthwise and thinly sliced (about 4 cups)
- 2 to 4 fresh jalapeno peppers, seeded, if desired, and chopped
- 4 cloves garlic, minced
- 1 teaspoon cumin seeds, crushed
- 2 15-ounce cans black-eyed peas, rinsed and drained
- ¼ cup sliced green onions
- 2 tablespoons snipped fresh cilantro or parsley
- ½ teaspoon salt
- 2 cups chopped tomatoes

1. In a large skillet, heat oil over medium heat. Add squash, peppers, garlic, and cumin; cook for 5 to 6 minutes or until squash is crisp-tender, stirring occasionally. Remove from heat; cool.

2. In a large bowl, combine squash mixture, black-eyed peas, green onions, cilantro, and salt. Cover and chill until serving time.

3. To serve, toss pea mixture with tomato. Makes 8 (¾-cup) servings.

Nutrition facts per serving: *161 calories, 5 g total fat, 1 g saturated fat, 0 mg cholesterol, 458 mg sodium, 24 g carbohydrate, 7 g fiber, 8 g protein.*

Lemon Pecan Pie

1   pastry for single-crust pie
3   slightly beaten eggs
5   tablespoons butter, melted
1½   cups sugar
6   tablespoons lemon juice
1   cup chopped pecans
     Lemon slices (optional)

1. Line a 9-inch pie plate with pastry; trim and crimp edge as desired.

2. Combine remaining ingredients; pour into pastry-lined pie plate.

3. To prevent overbrowning, cover edge of pie with foil. Bake in a 350°F. oven for 25 minutes. Remove foil. Bake for 20 to 25 minutes more or till set.

4. Cool on a wire rack. Refrigerate within 2 hours; cover for longer storage.

5. If desired, when serving, top each piece of pie with a twisted lemon slice. Makes 8 servings.

Nutrition facts per serving: *470 calories, 27 g fat, 8 g saturated fat, 99 mg cholesterol, 164 mg sodium, 55 g carbohydrate, 1 g fiber, 5 g protein, 10% DV Vitamin A, 9% DV Vitamin C, 1% DV calcium, 9% DV iron.*

Lemon Pecan Pie

perfect pork

The Machine Shed Stuffed Pork Loin with Sage Dressing

This meal contains some of the most popular dishes at The Machine Shed Restaurants. And with apple dumplings for dessert, you can be sure everyone will clean their plates!

The Machine Shed Stuffed Pork Loin with Sage Dressing

- 6   **cups dry bread cubes**
- 2   **celery stalks, sliced**
- 1   **medium onion, chopped (½ cup)**
- ¼   **cup butter**
- 1   **teaspoon dried sage, crushed**
- ½   **teaspoon salt**
- ½   **teaspoon poultry seasoning**
- ½   **teaspoon ground black pepper**
- ½   **cup chicken broth**
- 1   **2½-pound boneless pork top loin roast (single loin)**

1. Spread bread cubes in a shallow baking pan. Bake in a 350°F. oven for 10 to 12 minutes or until lightly toasted, stirring once or twice; set aside.

2. In a large skillet cook celery and onion in butter over medium heat until tender but not brown. Remove from heat. Stir in sage, salt, poultry seasoning, and pepper. Place bread cubes in a very large bowl; add vegetable mixture. Drizzle with enough chicken broth to moisten, tossing lightly to combine. Set stuffing aside.

3. To stuff pork, cut a lengthwise slit in the pork roast, cutting almost through the roast. Spoon some of the stuffing into the slit; tie roast closed with clean, 100% cotton kitchen string.

4. Place roast on a rack in a shallow roasting pan. Spoon any remaining stuffing around roast. Cover roast and stuffing with foil.

5. Roast for 1 hour. Remove foil. Roast for 35 to 45 minutes more or until internal temperature of meat registers 155°F. Cover and let stand 15 minutes (the meat's temperature will rise 5°F. during standing time). Remove string. Makes 8 servings.

THE
MACHINE SHED
A restaurant honoring the American farmer ®

FARMER'S FAVORITE

Try this dressing over a salad of greens, pears, candied walnuts and blue cheese.

Holiday Dijon Vinaigrette
Start to finish: 10 minutes

5   tablespoon extra-virgin olive oil
3   tablespoon finely chopped shallots
     or onions
2   tablespoon white wine vinegar
1   tablespoon Dijon-style mustard
½   teaspoon salt
¼   teaspoon ground black pepper

1. In a screw-top jar, combine all ingredients. Cover; shake well. Serve immediately. Or cover and store in refrigerator up to 1 week.

2. If refrigerated, let stand at room temperature 30 minutes before serving. Shake before serving over your favorite salad. Makes about ¾ cup.

Nutrition facts per serving: *81 calories, 9 g total fat, 1 g saturated fat, 7 g monounsaturated fat, 1 g polyunsaturated fat, 0 mg cholesterol, 191 mg sodium, 1 g carbohydrate, 0 g total sugar, 0 g fiber, 0 g protein, 1% DV Vitamin C, 1% DV iron.*

Better Homes and Gardens®
Test Kitchen

TEST KITCHEN TIP: TO ADD EXTRA ZIP, SUBSTITUTE SPICY MUSTARD FOR THE DIJON.

Holiday Dijon Vinaigrette

The Machine Shed Baked Potato Soup

The Machine Shed Baked Potato Soup

1½	pounds red potatoes, cut into ¾-inch cubes
6	slices bacon, chopped
1	medium onion, chopped
1	stalk celery, chopped
4	teaspoons all-purpose flour
4¾	cups chicken broth
2½	cups milk
½	teaspoon salt
½	teaspoon ground black pepper
½	cup butter or margarine
½	cup all-purpose flour
⅔	cup whipping cream
¼	cup snipped fresh parsley

1. Cook potatoes in a large saucepan in lightly salted boiling water for 10 to 12 minutes or until tender; drain and set aside.

2. In a 4-quart Dutch oven cook bacon, onion, and celery until bacon is crisp and onion is tender. Stir in 4 teaspoons flour. Add broth, milk, salt, and pepper. Cook and stir until just simmering (do not boil).

3. In a medium saucepan heat butter until melted. Stir in ½ cup flour. Cook and stir for 1 minute. Slowly add butter-flour mixture to milk mixture, stirring constantly. Cook and stir mixture until thickened and bubbly. Stir in cream and parsley. Stir in potatoes. Heat through. Garnish with shredded Colby cheese, crisp bacon pieces and fresh diced scallions if desired. Makes 8 servings.

THE MACHINE SHED
A restaurant honoring the American farmer ®

FARMER'S FAVORITE

Farm-Style Green Beans
Prep: 20 minutes   Cook: 10 minutes

1	pound green beans
4	slices bacon, cut up
1	cup sliced onion (2 medium)
2	cups chopped, seeded, peeled tomato (3 medium)
½	teaspoon salt

1. Remove ends and strings from green beans. Leave beans whole or cut into 1-inch pieces. Set aside.

2. In a large skillet cook bacon until crisp. Remove bacon, reserving 3 tablespoons drippings. Drain bacon on paper towels; set aside. Cook the onion in the reserved drippings over medium heat until tender. Add tomato and salt. Cook, uncovered, about 5 minutes more or until most of the liquid is absorbed.

3. Meanwhile, in a medium saucepan cook the beans in a small amount of boiling salted water for 10 to 15 minutes or until crisp-tender; drain. Transfer beans to a serving bowl. Top beans with the tomato mixture and bacon pieces. Makes 8 servings

Nutrition facts per serving: *99 calories, 7 g total fat, 2 g saturated fat, 3 g monounsaturated fat, 1 g polyunsaturated fat, 9 mg cholesterol, 244 mg sodium, 8 g carbohydrate, 3 g total sugar, 3 g fiber, 3 g protein, 24% DV Vitamin C, 3% DV calcium, 4% DV iron.*

Farm-Style Green Beans

Pine Nut-Parsley Rolls
Prep: 25 minutes   Rise: 30 minutes
Bake: 15 minutes

1	16-ounce package hot roll mix
1	cup warm water (120°F. to 130°F.)
2	tablespoons butter or margarine
1	egg
½	cup finely chopped pine nuts or slivered almonds
⅓	cup grated Parmesan cheese
¼	cup snipped fresh parsley
2	tablespoons butter or margarine, melted
1	slightly beaten egg
1	tablespoon water

1. Grease a baking sheet and set aside. Prepare roll mix according to package directions using the warm water, 2 tablespoons butter or margarine, and egg. Knead dough and let rest as directed on the package.

2. Combine pine nuts or almonds, cheese, and parsley. Roll dough on a lightly floured surface into an 18-inch square. Brush with 2 tablespoons melted butter or margarine; sprinkle with cheese mixture. Roll up dough; moisten and seal seam. Cut crosswise into twelve 1½-inch-thick slices.

3. Place slices, seam side down, on prepared baking sheet. Let rest for 5 minutes. Using a wooden spoon handle, press down in center of each slice to make a deep lengthwise crease on top of roll. Stir together slightly beaten egg and water; brush onto dough. Let rise in warm place until nearly double (30 to 35 minutes).

4. Bake in 375°F. oven about 15 minutes or until golden. Serve warm. Makes 12.

Nutrition facts per serving: *235 calories, 10 g total fat, 4 g saturated fat, 49 mg cholesterol, 325 mg sodium, 20 g carbohydrate, 0 g fiber, 9 g protein, 7% DV Vitamin A, 3% DV Vitamin C, 5% DV calcium, 10% DV iron.*

TEST KITCHEN TIP: TO MAKE AHEAD, BAKE AND COOL ROLLS. WRAP IN FOIL AND PLACE IN A LARGE PLASTIC FREEZER BAG OR FREEZER CONTAINER. SEAL, LABEL, AND FREEZE UP TO 1 MONTH. THAW OVERNIGHT IN REFRIGERATOR OR 2 HOURS AT ROOM TEMPERATURE. OR, PLACE FOIL-WRAPPED FROZEN ROLLS IN 325°F. OVEN FOR 20 MINUTES OR JUST UNTIL WARM.

Pine Nut-Parsley Rolls

The Machine Shed Apple Dumpling

Now that's cookin'!

The Machine Shed Apple Dumpling

3	cups water
1½	cups sugar
1	teaspoon ground cinnamon
⅓	cup butter
2⅔	cups all-purpose flour
½	teaspoon salt
¾	cup shortening
½ to ⅔	cup half-and-half, light cream, or whole milk
8	cooking apples, peeled and cored
8	teaspoons cinnamon-sugar
¼	cup butter, cut into 8 pieces

1. For sauce, in a large saucepan combine the water, 1½ cups sugar, and 1 teaspoon cinnamon. Bring to boiling, stirring to dissolve sugar. Remove from heat. Stir in ⅓ cup butter until melted. Set aside.

2. For pastry, in a large bowl combine the flour and salt. Using a pastry blender, cut in shortening until pieces are the size of small peas. Sprinkle 1 tablespoon of the cream over part of the mixture; gently toss with a fork. Push moistened dough to the side of the bowl. Repeat moistening dough, using 1 tablespoon of the cream at a time, until all of the dough is moistened. Form dough into a ball. Divide dough in half. On a lightly floured surface, roll each half of dough to a 12×12-inch rectangle. Cut each into four 6-inch squares.

3. Place an apple on each pastry square. Spoon 1 teaspoon cinnamon-sugar in the center of each. Place 1 piece of butter in the center of each. Moisten edges of each pastry square with water; fold corners to center over apple. Pinch to seal. Place in a 13×9×2-inch baking pan. Sprinkle with additional cinnamon-sugar, if desired.

4. Reheat sauce to boiling; pour over dumplings in pan. Bake, uncovered, in a 350°F. oven for 1 hour or until apples are tender and pastry is golden. To serve, spoon sauce over warm dumplings. Makes 8 servings.

THE MACHINE SHED
A restaurant honoring the American farmer ®

FARMER'S FAVORITE

family
classic

The Machine Shed Meatloaf

Nothing says "comfort food" like meatloaf. It tastes like home, and the best part is, it makes for fabulous sandwiches the next day … if there's any left, of course!

The Machine Shed Meatloaf

1	egg, lightly beaten
½	cup rolled oats
⅓	cup milk
¼	cup finely chopped onion
¼	cup finely chopped celery
¼	cup finely chopped green sweet pepper
¼	cup finely chopped red sweet pepper
¼	cup grated Parmesan cheese
1	tablespoon Worcestershire sauce
1	teaspoon salt
1	teaspoon garlic salt
1	teaspoon ground black pepper
1½	pounds ground beef
½	cup ketchup

1. In a large bowl combine egg, oats, milk, onion, celery, sweet peppers, Parmesan, Worcestershire, salt, garlic salt, and black pepper. Add meat; mix well. Lightly pat mixture into an 8×4×2-inch loaf pan.

2. Bake in a 350°F. oven for 1 to 1¼ hours or until internal temperature registers 160°F. Spoon off fat. Spread ketchup over meatloaf. Bake for 10 minutes more. Let stand 10 minutes before serving. Makes 8 servings.

The Machine Shed Garlic Mashed Potatoes

2	heads garlic
	Olive oil
8	medium baking potatoes (2½ to 3 pounds), peeled and quartered
¼	cup butter, softened
1	teaspoon salt
½	teaspoon ground black pepper
½	to ⅔ cup milk
¼	cup snipped fresh parsley

1. Peel away the dry outer layers of skin from garlic heads, leaving skins and cloves intact. Cut off the pointed top portion (about ¼ inch), leaving the bulbs intact but exposing the individual cloves. Place the garlic heads, cut sides up, in a small baking dish. Drizzle each with a little olive oil. Cover with foil and bake in a 425°F. oven for 25 to 35 minutes or until the cloves feel soft when pressed. Set aside just until cool enough to handle. Squeeze the garlic paste from the individual cloves; set paste aside.

2. Meanwhile, in a large saucepan cook potatoes, covered, in lightly salted boiling water for 20 to 25 minutes or until tender; drain. Mash with a potato masher or beat with an electric mixer on low speed. Add garlic paste, butter, salt, and pepper. Gradually beat in enough milk to make mixture light and fluffy. Stir in parsley. Makes 8 servings.

The Machine Shed Garlic Mashed Potatoes

Basil Peas and Mushrooms
Start to finish: 25 minutes

- ½ cup sliced carrot (1 medium)
- 1 10-ounce package frozen peas
- 2 cups sliced mushrooms
- 2 green onions, cut into ½-inch pieces
- 1 tablespoon butter or margarine
- 1 tablespoon snipped fresh basil or ½ teaspoon dried basil, crushed
- ¼ teaspoon salt
  Dash black pepper

1. In a medium saucepan cook carrot, covered, in a small amount of boiling salted water for 3 minutes. Add the peas. Return to boiling; reduce heat. Cook about 5 minutes more or until carrot and peas are crisp-tender. Drain well. Remove carrot and peas from saucepan; set aside.

2. In the same saucepan cook mushrooms and green onion in hot butter until tender. Stir in basil, salt, and pepper. Return carrot and peas to saucepan; heat through. Makes 6 servings.

Nutrition facts per serving: *69 calories, 3 g total fat, 1 g saturated fat, 1 g monounsaturated fat, 0 g polyunsaturated fat, 5 mg cholesterol, 171 mg sodium, 9 g carbohydrate, 4 g total sugar, 3 g fiber, 4 g protein, 13% DV Vitamin C, 2% DV calcium, 6% DV iron.*

Basil Peas and Mushrooms

Creamed Corn Casserole

Creamed Corn Casserole

Prep: 15 minutes   Bake: 50 minutes

Nonstick cooking spray
2 **16-ounce packages frozen whole kernel corn**
2 **cups chopped red and/or green sweet pepper**
1 **cup chopped onion (1 large)**
1 **tablespoon butter or margarine**
¼ **teaspoon black pepper**
1 **10.75-ounce can condensed cream of celery soup**
1 **8-ounce tub cream cheese spread with chive and onion or cream cheese spread with garden vegetables**
¼ **cup milk**

1. Lightly coat a 2-quart casserole with cooking spray; set aside. Place corn in a colander and thaw by running under cool water; drain. Set aside.

2. In a large saucepan cook sweet pepper and onion in 1 tablespoon hot butter until tender. Stir in corn and black pepper. In a medium bowl whisk together soup, cream cheese spread, and milk. Stir soup mixture into corn mixture. Transfer to prepared casserole.

3. Bake, covered, in a 375°F. oven for 50 to 55 minutes or until heated through, stirring once. Makes 12 servings

Slow cooker directions: Do not thaw corn and omit butter. In a 3½- or 4-quart slow cooker combine frozen corn, sweet peppers, onion, and black pepper. In a medium bowl whisk together celery soup, cream cheese, and milk. Pour over mixture in cooker. Cover and cook on low-heat setting for 8 to 10 hours or on high-heat setting for 4 to 5 hours. Stir before serving.

Nutrition facts per serving: *176 calories, 9 g total fat, 5 g saturated fat, 1 g monounsaturated fat, 0 g polyunsaturated fat, 22 mg cholesterol, 280 sodium, 22 g carbohydrate, 5 g total sugar, 3 g fiber, 4 g protein, 38% DV Vitamin C, 4% calcium, 3% DV iron.*

Cranberry Waldorf Salad
Start to finish: 30 minutes

- 4 cups chopped pears or chopped apples
- 1 cup seedless grapes, halved
- 1 cup sliced celery
- ⅔ cup slivered almonds or broken pecans, toasted
- ½ cup snipped pitted whole dates or raisins
  Leaf lettuce
- ⅔ cup whole cranberry sauce
- ¼ cup mayonnaise or salad dressing
- ¼ cup dairy sour cream
- ¼ cup milk
- 2 teaspoons lemon juice
- ¼ teaspoon celery seed

1. In a medium mixing bowl, combine chopped pears or apples, grapes, celery, almonds or pecans, and dates or raisins. Divide fruit mixture among lettuce-lined salad plates.

2. For dressing, in a small mixing bowl, combine cranberry sauce, mayonnaise or salad dressing, sour cream, milk, lemon juice, and celery seed. Drizzle dressing over fruit mixture. Makes 10 to 12 servings.

Nutrition facts per serving: *211 calories, 11 g total fat, 2 g saturated fat, 5 mg cholesterol, 49 mg sodium, 29 g carbohydrate, 4 g fiber, 3 g protein, 10% DV Vitamin C, 5% DV calcium, 5% DV iron.*

Better Homes and Gardens
Test Kitchen

TEST KITCHEN TIP: TO MAKE AHEAD, ONE DAY BEFORE SERVING, STIR TOGETHER SALAD DRESSING; COVER AND CHILL OVERNIGHT. TOAST NUTS; COOL, COVER AND CHILL OVERNIGHT.

Caramelized Upside-Down Pear Ginger Cake

Prep: 20 minutes   Bake: 30 minutes
Cool: 5 minutes   Stand: 5 minutes

¾   cup packed brown sugar
¼   cup butter
2   tablespoons light-colored corn syrup
1   teaspoon vanilla
½   cup chopped pecans,
       toasted (optional)
3   medium firm Bosc pears
1   2-layer-size package spice cake mix
1   egg
1   tablespoon finely chopped
       crystallized ginger
       Vanilla ice cream
       Purchased caramel sauce,
       warmed (optional)

1. Preheat oven to 350°F. In a medium skillet, combine the brown sugar, butter, and corn syrup. Cook and stir over medium heat until combined. Remove from heat; stir in vanilla. Divide mixture evenly between two 9×1½-inch round cake pans. Sprinkle with nuts, if using.

2. Core pears and, if desired, peel pears. Cut into thin wedges. Arrange pears in the pans. Set aside.

3. Prepare cake mix according to package directions, except add the 1 additional egg. Stir in finely chopped crystallized ginger. Spoon batter evenly over pear slices in pans.

4. Bake in preheated oven for 30 to 35 minutes or until a toothpick inserted near centers comes out clean. Cool in pans on wire racks for 5 minutes. Loosen cakes from sides of pans; invert onto serving platters. Serve warm with ice cream and, if desired, warmed caramel sauce. Makes 16 servings.

Nutrition facts per serving: *285 calories, 11 g total fat, 3 g saturated fat, 62 mg cholesterol, 249 mg sodium, 44 g carbohydrate, 1 g fiber, 3 b protein, 2% DV Vitamin C, 7% DV calcium, 2% DV iron.*

Caramelized Upside-Down Pear Ginger Cake

sit-down dinner

This is a wonderful meal to make when you have a busy day but still want to have a nice dinner. Nearly everything can be prepared ahead of time.

The Machine Shed Old-Fashioned Pot Roast

The Machine Shed Old-Fashioned Pot Roast

1	2½- to 3-pound boneless beef chuck pot roast
2	tablespoons cooking oil
1	large onion, quartered
¾	cup beef broth
1	tablespoon Worcestershire sauce

1. Trim fat from meat. In a 4- to 6-quart Dutch oven brown roast on all sides in hot oil. Drain off fat. Add onion to pan. Stir together broth and Worcestershire sauce and pour over beef. Bring to boiling.

2. Cover and bake in a 325°F. oven for 2 to 3 hours or until meat is very tender. Makes 8 servings.

THE MACHINE SHED
A restaurant honoring the American farmer ®

FARMER'S FAVORITE

Glorious Greens with Hazelnut Vinaigrette

- 1 recipe Hazelnut Vinaigrette (see recipe below)
- 2 heads butter lettuce, bibb lettuce, and/or Boston lettuce
- 1 cup chopped Roma tomatoes
- ½ cup finely sliced red onion slivers
- ¼ cup coarsely chopped toasted hazelnuts
- 1 ounce manchego cheese or Parmesan cheese, finely shredded

1. Prepare hazelnut vinaigrette. Set aside. (Vinaigrette can be made a day ahead. Whisk before using.)

2. Separate leaves from each head of lettuce. Each individual salad requires 5 leaves, ranging in size from about 4 inches in diameter to 1½ inches in diameter.

3. To compose salad, on each of 4 individual plates, layer the largest leaf (about 4 inches), a few chopped tomatoes, a few red onion slivers, a sprinkling of nuts, and a drizzle of Hazelnut Vinaigrette. Repeat layering, stacking carefully, until all of the lettuce leaves are used. Top each serving with finely shredded manchego or Parmesan cheese. Makes 4 salads.

Hazelnut Vinaigrette: In a small bowl whisk together 3 tablespoons champagne vinegar or white wine vinegar, 1 tablespoon finely chopped shallots, ½ teaspoon salt, and ¼ teaspoon pepper. Slowly whisk in 3 tablespoons hazelnut oil.

Nutrition facts per serving: *199 calories, 17 g total fat, 2 g saturated fat, 6 mg cholesterol, 374 mg sodium, 7 g carbohydrate, 2 g fiber, 5 g protein, 23% DV Vitamin C, 9% DV calcium, 5% DV iron.*

Herbed Roasted Vegetables
Prep: 15 minutes   Roast: 35 minutes

- 2 medium sweet potatoes or white potatoes, cut into 1-inch cubes (about 12 ounces)
- 2 carrots, cut into 1-inch chunks
- 1 medium parsnip, peeled and cut into 1-inch pieces
- 1 medium red onion, quartered
- 1 tablespoon olive oil
- 3 cloves garlic, minced
- 2 teaspoons dried mixed herbs (such as marjoram, thyme, rosemary, and oregano), crushed
- ¼ teaspoon salt
- ¼ teaspoon pepper

1. Place potatoes, carrots, parsnip, and red onion in a 13×9×2-inch baking pan. Combine oil, garlic, mixed herbs, salt, and pepper. Drizzle over vegetables, tossing to coat.

2. Cover with foil. Bake in a 425°F. oven for 30 minutes. Remove foil; stir vegetables. Bake, uncovered, for 5 to 10 minutes more or until vegetables are tender. Makes 6 servings.

Nutrition facts per serving: *113 calories, 3 g total fat, 0 g saturated fat, 0 mg cholesterol, 116 mg sodium, 22 g carbohydrate, 4 g fiber, 2 g protein, 172% DV Vitamin A, 26% DV Vitamin C, 4% DV calcium, 7% DV iron.*

Glorious Greens with Hazelnut Vinaigrette

Herbed Roasted Vegetables

Mama's Dinner Rolls

Mama's
Dinner Rolls

Prep: 40 minutes   Rise: 1¾ hour   Bake: 20 minutes

¼	cup warm water (105° to 115°F.)
2	packages active dry yeast
1	cup milk
1	cup butter
1	cup sugar
½	teaspoon salt
3	eggs
6	to 6½ cups all-purpose flour
2	tablespoons butter, melted

1. Stir together the warm water and yeast. Set aside.

2. In a medium saucepan, heat and stir milk, 1 cup butter, the sugar, and salt just until warm (120° to 130°F.) and butter almost melts. In a very large bowl, combine milk mixture, yeast mixture, and eggs. Stir in 4½ cups flour. Cover and let rise in a warm place until nearly double (1 to 1½ hours). Stir dough down. Using a wooden spoon, stir in as much of the remaining flour as you can.

3. Turn the dough out onto a floured surface. Knead in enough of the remaining flour to make a moderately soft dough that is smooth and elastic (3 to 5 minutes total). Cover and let rest for 10 minutes. (Dough will be soft.)

4. Brush three 9×1½-inch round baking pans with some of the melted butter; set aside. On a lightly floured surface, roll dough to ½-inch thickness. Using a 2½-inch round cutter, cut dough into about 30 rounds, re-rolling dough as necessary. Brush rounds with remaining melted butter.

5. Fold each round nearly in half, buttered side inside, so that the top slightly overlaps the bottom. Divide rolls evenly among the prepared pans. Cover; let rise in a warm place until almost double (about 45 minutes).

6. Bake in a 350°F. oven about 20 minutes or until golden. Invert onto wire racks to cool slightly; serve warm. Makes about 30 rolls.

Nutrition Facts per roll: *182 calories, 8 g total fat, 5 g saturated fat, 40 mg cholesterol, 116 mg sodium, 25 g carbohydrate, 1 g dietary fiber, 4 g protein.*

Raspberry Pear Jam

Start to finish: 1 hour

- 6 ripe medium pears, peeled, cored, and cut up
- 4 cups fresh raspberries
- 3 tablespoons lemon juice
- 1 1¾-ounce package powdered fruit pectin
- 6 cups sugar

1. Place pears in a large mixing bowl. Use a potato masher or fork to break the pears into small pieces. Measure the pears. You should have 2½ cups of mashed pears. Place the raspberries in another bowl and mash into small pieces.

2. Measure the sugar and set it aside until you need it. Combine the mashed pears and raspberries, the lemon juice, and the powdered fruit pectin in a 6- to 8-quart Dutch oven or kettle. Bring to boiling over high heat, stirring constantly. Stir in the sugar. Bring to a full rolling boil. A full rolling boil is one that cannot be stirred down. Boil the mixture hard for 1 minute, stirring constantly, using a long-handled wooden spoon. Remove the Dutch oven from the heat. Use a metal spoon to skim off the foam.

3. To fill the jars, place a wide-mouth plastic funnel in a sterilized, hot half-pint canning jar. Ladle the jam into the hot jar, leaving ¼ inch of space at the top of the jar. Remove the funnel and wipe the jar rim with a clean, damp paper towel. Food on the rim prevents a perfect seal. Position a prepared lid and screw band on the jar and tighten according to the manufacturer's directions. As you fill each jar, place it in boiling water in a water-bath canner. The jars should not touch one another. Cover the canner. Begin the processing time when the water returns to boiling. Process the jam for 5 minutes. Remove jars from canner and cool on a wire rack. Makes 8 half-pints (111 1-tablespoon servings).

Nutrition facts per serving: *49 calories, 0 g total fat, 0 g saturated fat, 0 mg cholesterol, 1 mg sodium, 13 g carbohydrate, 1 g fiber, 0 g protein, 3% DV Vitamin C.*

Raspberry Pear Jam

TEST KITCHEN TIP: WHEN THE JARS HAVE COOLED, PRESS THE CENTER OF EACH LID TO CHECK THE SEAL. IF THE DIP IN THE LID HOLDS, THE JAR IS SEALED. IF THE LID BOUNCES UP AND DOWN, THE JAR ISN'T SEALED. IF YOU HAVE A JAR THAT HAS NOT SEALED, YOU CAN STORE THE JAM IN THE REFRIGERATOR FOR UP TO 3 WEEKS. LABEL THE SEALED JARS WITH THE CONTENT AND DATE. STORE IN A COOL, DRY PLACE FOR 1 YEAR.

Better Homes and Gardens
Test Kitchen

Grandma's Berry-Apple Pie

Pastry for double-crust pie
1   cup sugar
4   teaspoons quick-cooking tapioca
½   teaspoon ground cinnamon
2   cups fresh blackberries
2   cups sliced, peeled apples
2   tablespoons butter, cut up

1. Prepare pastry and divide in half. Form each half into a ball. On a lightly floured surface, roll one ball of the pastry into a 12-inch circle. Transfer the rolled-out pastry onto a 9-inch pie plate.

2. In large mixing bowl, stir together the sugar, tapioca and cinnamon. Add the blackberries and apple slices. Toss gently till coated. Let stand 15 minutes.

3. Spoon filling into pastry-lined pie plate. Dot with butter. Trim pastry even with edge of the pie plate. Moisten the edge of the pastry with water.

4. On a lightly floured surface, roll out the remaining pastry into a 12-inch circle. Cut slits in the pastry to let steam escape. Place pastry on the filling. Trim the top crust to half inch beyond edge of pie plate. Fold top pastry and crimp edge. Cover edge of crust with foil to prevent overbrowning.

5. Bake in a 375° oven for 25 minutes. Remove the foil. Bake for 20 to 25 minutes more or till the crust is golden brown and the filling is bubbly. Cool on a wire rack. Makes 8 servings.

Nutrition facts per serving: 419 calories, 21 g. fat, 57 g. carbohydrate, 3 g. protein, 8 mg. cholesterol, 3 g. fiber, 165 mg. sodium.

Grandma's Berry-Apple Pie

holiday
or any day

Make this meal for a holiday or special occasion, or show your family

that every meal with them is special, and surprise them on a Tuesday!

The Machine Shed French Onion Soup

The Machine Shed French Onion Soup

- 6 onions, thinly sliced
- 3 tablespoons butter
- ¼ cup sugar
- 4 14-ounce cans beef broth
- 1 cup dry red wine

1. In a 4-quart Dutch oven cook onions in hot butter over medium heat for 15 minutes or until tender, stirring occasionally. Stir in sugar the last 5 minutes of cooking.

2. Stir in the broth and wine. Heat through. Garnish individual servings with one slice of French bread, add Swiss cheese, melt, and top with onion rings, if desired. Makes 8 servings.

FARMER'S FAVORITE

Hazelnut-Crusted Turkey Breast

Hazelnut-Crusted Turkey Breast

Prep: 20 minutes   Roast: 1½ hours

- 1   3- to 3½-pound turkey breast half with bone
- 1   tablespoon olive oil or cooking oil
- 1   clove garlic, minced
- ¼   teaspoon salt
- ½   cup hazelnuts (filberts)
- ½   teaspoon ground coriander
- ¼   teaspoon coarsely ground black pepper
- ⅛   teaspoon ground cinnamon
- ¼   cup orange marmalade
   Oranges, halved (optional)
   Kumquats (optional)
   Fresh bay leaves (optional)

1. Preheat oven to 375°F. Remove skin from turkey breast. Place turkey breast on a lightly greased rack in a shallow roasting pan. In a small bowl, combine oil, garlic, and salt. Brush oil mixture over turkey breast. Insert a meat thermometer into the thickest portion of the breast. (The thermometer should not touch bone.) Roast for 45 minutes.

2. Meanwhile, place hazelnuts in a blender or food processor. Cover and blend or process until finely chopped. Transfer nuts to a small bowl; stir in coriander, pepper, and cinnamon. Set aside.

3. Remove turkey breast from oven. Brush surface with orange marmalade. Sprinkle with nut mixture; press gently so nuts adhere to the turkey breast. Continue roasting for 45 to 60 minutes more or until thermometer registers 170°F. Remove from oven.

4. Cover and let turkey breast stand for 15 minutes. Place turkey breast on a serving platter; slice turkey. If desired, garnish with oranges, kumquats, and bay leaves. Makes 6 to 8 servings.

Nutrition facts per serving: 260 calories, 8 g total fat, 88 mg cholesterol, 58 mg sodium, 9 g carbohydrate, 1 g fiber, 38 g protein, 1% DV Vitamin C, 4% DV calcium, 14% DV iron.

Cheesy Wild Rice Casserole

Prep: 20 minutes   Bake: 35 minutes

- 1   6-ounce package long grain and wild rice mix
- 1   4-ounce can sliced mushrooms, drained
- 2½ cups water
- 1   10-ounce package frozen chopped spinach
- ¾   cup chopped onion
- 1   tablespoon butter or margarine
- 2   teaspoons prepared mustard
- ¼   teaspoon ground nutmeg
- 1   8-ounce package cream cheese, cut into cubes

1. In a 2-quart casserole, combine rice mix and seasoning packet with mushrooms. In a medium saucepan, combine water, spinach, onion, butter, mustard, and nutmeg. Bring to boiling; remove from heat. Stir mixture; pour over rice mixture. Stir in cream cheese.

2. Bake, covered, in a 375°F. oven 20 minutes. Stir mixture. Cover; bake 15 to 20 minutes more or until rice is tender. Stir again. Let stand 5 minutes before serving. Makes 6 to 8 servings.

Nutrition facts per serving: *271 calories, 16 g total fat, 10 g saturated fat, 47 mg cholesterol, 692 mg sodium, 26 mg carbohydrate, 3 g fiber, 7 g protein.*

TEST KITCHEN TIP: THIS RICE DISH TASTES JUST AS CREAMY WHEN YOU MAKE IT WITH REDUCED-FAT CREAM CHEESE (NEUFCHATEL). THE CASSEROLE CAN BE ASSEMBLED AHEAD AND REFRIGERATED FOR UP TO 2 HOURS BEFORE BAKING. ADD A FEW EXTRA MINUTES TO THE BAKING TIME TO HEAT THE CASSEROLE THROUGH.

Better Homes and Gardens Test Kitchen

Cheesy Wild Rice Casserole

Broccoli and Peppers with Walnuts
Start to finish: 25 minutes

¼   cup chicken broth
2   tablespoons oyster sauce
1   teaspoon finely shredded lemon peel
⅛   teaspoon cayenne pepper
4   teaspoons cooking oil
½   cup coarsely chopped walnuts
1   clove garlic, minced
1   pound broccoli, cut into 1-inch florets
1   medium red sweet pepper, cut into
    bite-size strips

1. For sauce, in a small bowl combine chicken broth, oyster sauce, lemon peel, and cayenne pepper; set aside.

2. In a large nonstick skillet heat 2 teaspoons of the oil over medium heat. Add walnuts and garlic; cook and stir for 2 to 3 minutes or until nuts are lightly toasted. Remove the walnut mixture from the skillet; set mixture aside.

3. In the same skillet heat the remaining oil over medium-high heat. Add broccoli and sweet pepper; cook and stir for 2 to 3 minutes or until vegetables are crisp-tender.

4. Stir sauce; add to skillet. Cook and stir for 1 minute. Transfer mixture to serving bowl. Sprinkle with walnut mixture. Makes 6 servings

Nutrition facts per serving: *133 calories, 10 g total fat, 1 g saturated fat, 2 g monounsaturated fat, 6 g polyunsaturated fat, 0 mg cholesterol, 299 mg sodium, 10 g carbohydrate, 4 g total sugar, 3 g fiber, 4 g protein, 150% DV Vitamin C, 5% DV calcium, 7% DV iron.*

Broccoli and Peppers with Walnuts

Pumpkin Gingerbread Pie

Maple-Orange Sweet Potatoes and Carrots

Prep: 20 minutes
Cook: 8 hours on low or 4 hours on high

Nonstick cooking spray
1   16-ounce package peeled baby carrots
2   pounds sweet potatoes, peeled and cut into 1½-inch pieces
1   cup snipped dried apricots
½   cup pure maple syrup or maple-flavored syrup
¼   cup frozen orange juice concentrate, thawed
¼   cup water
2   tablespoons butter or margarine, melted
½   teaspoon salt
¼   teaspoon ground white pepper
¼   teaspoon ground cinnamon

1. Lightly coat a 3½- or 4-quart slow cooker with cooking spray. In the cooker layer carrots, sweet potatoes, and dried apricots.
2. In a small bowl combine maple syrup, orange juice concentrate, water, melted butter, salt, white pepper, and cinnamon. Pour over mixture in cooker.
3. Cover; cook on low-heat setting for 8 to 9 hours or on high-heat setting for 4 to 4½ hours. Use a slotted spoon to serve. Makes 10 side-dish servings.

Nutrition facts per serving: *194 calories, 3 g total fat, 2 g saturated fat, 1 g monounsaturated fat, 0 g polyunsaturated fat, 7 mg cholesterol, 168 mg sodium, 42 g carbohydrate, 23 g total sugar, 5 g fiber, 2 g protein, 41% DV Vitamin C, 5% DV calcium, 8% DV iron.*

Pumpkin Gingerbread Pie

Prep: 25 minutes   Bake: 50 minutes

Nonstick cooking spray
1   cup canned pumpkin
⅓   cup sugar
1   teaspoon pumpkin pie spice
1   slightly beaten egg
½   cup half-and-half or light cream
1   14.5-oz. package gingerbread mix
    Whipped cream (optional)

1. Preheat oven to 350°F. Coat a 10-inch deep-dish pie plate or an 8×8×2-inch baking dish with cooking spray; set aside. In a small mixing bowl combine pumpkin, sugar, and pumpkin pie spice. Add egg. Beat lightly with a rotary beater or fork just until combined. Gradually stir in half-and-half; mix well.
2. Prepare gingerbread mix according to package directions. Pour batter into prepared pie plate or dish. Lightly spoon pumpkin mixture over gingerbread batter; swirl gently using a table knife. Bake for 50 minutes for pie plate or 60 minutes for baking dish or until a pick inserted in gingerbread portion comes out clean. Cool slightly. Serve warm or at room temperature with whipped cream. Makes 8 servings.

Nutrition facts per serving: *304 calories, 10 g total fat, 3 g saturated fat, 5 g monounsaturated fat, 1 g polyunsaturated fat, 58 mg cholesterol, 364 mg sodium, 50 g carbohydrate, 33 g total sugar, 2 g fiber, 5 g protein, 3% DV Vitamin C, 8% DV calcium, 17% DV iron.*

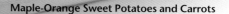

Maple-Orange Sweet Potatoes and Carrots

FRONT-PORCH *fare*

Not every meal on the farm is a
sit-at-the-table, four-course affair.
Sometimes, all you really need is a porch swing, a little bite to eat,
a refreshing drink, and your sweetheart at your side.

Maybe it's too late for a full meal. Maybe it's too hot. Or maybe you're
just too tired. If farm wives served the kinds of meals featured in this
cookbook three times a day, they wouldn't have time for anything else.

And goodness knows, there's plenty else to do.

*Pull up a porch swing,
listen to the crickets,
relax, and enjoy!*

Citrus Snack

This mini-meal is satisfying without being too heavy.

Ham, Cheese and Fruit We

Ham, Cheese and Fruit Wedges

Prep: 20 minutes   Bake: 12 minutes

- ¾   cup mixed dried fruit bits (about ½ of a 6-ounce package)
- ½   cup finely chopped cooked ham
- ½   cup finely chopped walnuts
- ½   cup shredded fontina cheese (2 ounces)
- 1   15-ounce package folded refrigerated pie crust (2 crusts)
      Milk
- ¼   teaspoon poppy seeds

1. For filling, stir together fruit bits, ham, walnuts, and cheese in a mixing bowl.

2. Unfold pie crusts on a lightly floured surface according to package directions. Transfer one crust to a large ungreased cookie sheet. Sprinkle filling evenly over crust to about 1 inch of the edge. Brush edge with milk; top with second crust. Flute edge of pastry or press with fork to seal. Cut slits or make small cutouts in top pastry to allow steam to escape. Brush top with milk; sprinkle with poppy seeds.

3. Bake in a 425°F. oven for 12 to 15 minutes or until golden. Cool slightly on a wire rack. Cut into wedges, and serve warm. Makes 16 servings.

Nutrition facts per serving: *180 calories, 11 g total fat, 4 g saturated fat, 11 mg cholesterol, 199 mg sodium, 18 g carbohydrate, 0 g fiber, 3 g protein, 1% DV Vitamin A, 3% DV calcium, 1% DV iron.*

Citrus-Mint Drink

Citrus-Mint Drink

Prep: 15 minutes   Chill: 4 hours

- 1   cup snipped fresh mint leaves
- 2   cups water
- ⅔   cup sugar
- 1   teaspoon shredded orange peel
- 2   cups orange juice
- ⅔   cup lemon juice
     Cracked ice
     Fresh mint sprigs (optional)

Place mint leaves in a medium bowl. Bring water and sugar to boiling in a small saucepan, stirring until sugar dissolves. Remove from heat; pour over mint leaves. Stir in orange peel, orange juice, and lemon juice. Cover; let stand at room temperature for 1 hour. Strain. Cover and chill for 4 to 24 hours. Serve over ice. If desired, garnish with mint sprigs. Makes eight 4-ounce servings.

Nutrition facts per serving: *98 calories, 0 g total fat, 0 g saturated fat, 0 mg cholesterol, 3 mg sodium, 25 g carbohydrate, 0 g fiber, 1 g protein, 4% DV Vitamin A, 79% DV Vitamin C, 2% DV calcium, 11% DV iron.*

Chilled Lemony Pea Soup

Prep: 5 minutes   Chill: 1 hour
Cook: 8 minutes

- 2   teaspoons olive oil
- ¼   cup sliced green onion
- 1   14-ounce can reduced-sodium chicken broth
- 2   teaspoons cornstarch
- 2   cups shelled fresh peas or one 10-ounce package frozen peas, thawed
- 1   tablespoon snipped fresh mint
- 1   tablespoon freshly squeezed lemon juice
      Lemon slices

1. Heat olive oil in a medium saucepan. Cook and stir green onion over medium heat for 30 seconds or until soft. Add all but 2 tablespoons of the chicken broth. Bring to boiling; reduce heat. Cook, covered, over medium-low heat for 5 minutes.

2. Stir cornstarch and remaining broth together in a small bowl until smooth. Add cornstarch mixture to saucepan. Cook and stir until slightly thickened and bubbly; cook and stir 2 minutes more. Remove from heat. Stir in peas and mint. Let mixture cool slightly.

3. Transfer pea mixture to a blender container or food processor bowl. Cover and blend or process until smooth. Transfer mixture to a bowl. Cover and chill thoroughly (at least 1 hour). To serve, stir in lemon juice and garnish with lemon slices. Makes 4 servings.

Nutrition facts per serving: *93 calories, 3 g total fat, 0 g saturated fat, 0 mg cholesterol, 276 mg sodium, 13 g carbohydrate, 4 g fiber, 5 g protein, 47% DV Vitamin C, 2% DV calcium, 8% DV iron.*

Chilled Lemony Pea Soup

Keep it cool

Light and refreshing, this is a perfect meal for a hot summer day.

Cool-as-a-Cucumber Chicken Salad

Cool-as-a-Cucumber Chicken Salad

Start to finish: 25 minutes

2	cups cubed cantaloupe and/or honeydew melon
1	cup finely chopped cucumber
1	cup finely chopped zucchini
¼	cup thinly sliced green onions
⅓	cup lime juice
2	tablespoons salad oil
2	tablespoons water
2	tablespoons snipped fresh cilantro or mint
1	tablespoon sugar
⅛	teaspoon ground white pepper
4	cups shredded leaf lettuce
2	cups shredded cooked chicken (10 ounces)

1. In a large bowl, toss together the cantaloupe, cucumber, zucchini, and green onions.

2. For dressing, in a screw-top jar, combine lime juice, oil, water, cilantro, sugar, and white pepper. Cover and shake well. Drizzle ½ cup of the dressing over the melon mixture. Toss lightly to coat.

3. Divide shredded lettuce among four dinner plates. Top with the melon mixture. Arrange chicken around edges of plates. Drizzle remaining dressing over chicken. Makes 4 main-dish servings.

Nutrition facts per serving: *258 calories, 12 g total fat, 3 g saturated fat, 62 mg cholesterol, 77 mg sodium, 16 g carbohydrate, 3 g fiber, 22 g protein.*

Watermelon-Berry Sorbet

Watermelon-Berry Sorbet

Prep: 25 minutes   Freeze: 2½ hours

- 1   cup water
- ½   cup sugar
- 2   cups seeded watermelon cubes
- 2   cups fresh berries (raspberries, strawberries, and/or blueberries)
  Snipped fresh lemon balm
  Fresh lemon balm sprigs
  Fresh raspberries and/or blueberries (optional)

1. In a medium saucepan combine water and sugar; bring to boiling, stirring frequently. Boil gently, uncovered, for 2 minutes. Remove from heat and cool slightly.

2. Place the watermelon and berries in a blender or large food processor; cover and blend or process for 30 seconds. Add the warm syrup and blend until almost smooth. Transfer the mixture to a 3-quart rectangular baking dish or a 13×9×2-inch baking pan. Place in the freezer, uncovered, for 1½ hours or until almost solid.

3. Remove sorbet from freezer. Using a fork, break up the frozen fruit into a somewhat smooth mixture. Stir in snipped lemon balm. Freeze 1 hour more. Break up the ice with a fork and serve in shallow bowls. Top with lemon balm sprigs and a few blueberries and/or raspberries. Note: If mixture is frozen longer than the final hour, let it stand at room temperature about 20 minutes before breaking up mixture with a fork and serving.

Nutrition facts per serving: *98 calories, 0 g total fat, 0 g saturated fat, 2 mg sodium, 24 g carbohydrate, 24 g total sugar, 3 g fiber, 1 g protein, 25% DV Vitamin C, 1% DV calcium, 2% DV iron.*

Refreshing Iced Tea

Prep: 20 minutes   Chill: 4 hours
Cook: 5 minutes

- 7   cups water
- 2   cups sugar
- 8   tea bags orange pekoe tea
- 8   sprigs fresh mint
- 8   cups cold water
- 2   cups orange juice
- ¾   cup lemon juice
      Ice cubes
      Fresh mint sprigs (optional)

1. In a large saucepan combine the 7 cups water and 2 cups sugar. Bring to boiling, stirring to dissolve sugar; reduce heat. Simmer, uncovered, for 5 minutes. Remove from heat. Add tea bags and 8 mint sprigs; cover and let stand for 5 minutes. Using a slotted spoon, remove tea bags and mint sprigs; discard.

2. Transfer tea to a heatproof 1½- to 2-gallon bowl or container. Add the 8 cups cold water, orange juice, and lemon juice. Cover and refrigerate at least 4 hours or up to 2 days. Serve tea over ice and garnish with additional mint sprigs. Makes 16 to 18 eight-ounce servings.

Nutrition facts per serving: *110 calories, 0 g total fat, 0 g saturated fat, 0 mg cholesterol, 3 mg sodium, 28 g carbohydrate, 24 g total sugar, 0 g fiber, 0 g protein, 37% DV Vitamin C, 1% DV calcium, 3% DV iron.*

Better Homes and Gardens Test Kitchen

TEST KITCHEN TIP: YOU CAN HALVE THIS RECIPE IF YOU WANT FEWER SERVINGS.

Refreshing Iced Tea

Fresh from the Garden

Use fruit and veggies from your garden or the farmer's market for this meal.

Fruit Kabobs

Fruit Kabobs

Prep: 20 minutes   Chill: 30 to 60 minutes

- ¾ cup cantaloupe chunks
- ¾ cup honeydew melon chunks
- ¾ cup small strawberries
- ¾ cup pineapple chunks
- 2 small bananas, peeled and cut into 1-inch slices
- 1 cup orange juice
- ¼ cup lime juice
- 1 8-ounce carton vanilla low-fat or fat-free yogurt
- 2 tablespoons frozen orange juice concentrate, thawed
  Ground nutmeg or ground cinnamon (optional)

1. On eight 6-inch or four 10-inch skewers alternately thread the cantaloupe, honeydew melon, strawberries, pineapple, and bananas. Place kabobs in a glass baking dish. Combine orange juice and lime juice; pour evenly over kabobs. Cover; chill kabobs for 30 to 60 minutes, turning occasionally.

2. Meanwhile, for dip, in a small bowl stir together the yogurt and orange juice concentrate. Cover and chill until ready to serve.

3. To serve, arrange the kabobs on a serving platter; discard juice mixture. If desired, sprinkle nutmeg or cinnamon over dip. Serve dip with kabobs. Makes 8 servings.

Nutrition facts per serving: *91 calories, 1 g total fat, 0 g saturated fat, 2 mg cholesterol, 20 mg sodium, 21 g carbohydrate, 1 g fiber, 2 g protein, 6% DV Vitamin A, 78% DV Vitamin C, 4% DV calcium, 2% DV iron.*

All Wrapped Up Chef Salad
Prep: 20 minutes   Chill: 30 minutes

1   cup Thousand Island dressing
2   tablespoons chopped, bottled, pickled
     jalapeno peppers
4   burrito-size flour tortillas
3   cups torn romaine lettuce
½   pound sliced deli roast beef
½   pound sliced deli turkey breast
1   medium-size tomato, thinly sliced
1   avocado, pitted, peeled, sliced
½   seedless cucumber, thinly sliced
1   cup shredded pepper-Jack cheese

1. In cup, mix dressing, jalapeno. Spread 2 tablespoons over each tortilla. Scatter romaine over each.

2. Layer beef, turkey, tomato, avocado, cucumber on each tortilla. Sprinkle ¼ cup cheese over each. Tightly roll up each tortilla. Wrap in damp paper toweling; refrigerate at least 30 minutes or up to 1 hour.

3. Remove toweling. Halve each diagonally. Serve dressing on side. Makes 8 servings.

Nutrition facts per serving: *390 calories, 23 g total fat, 7 g saturated fat, 48 mg cholesterol, 1111 mg sodium, 30 g carbohydrate, 4 g sugar, 18 g protein.*

Strawberry Iced Tea
Prep: 25 minutes   Cool: 2 hours
Stand: 2 hours

2   lb. fresh strawberries or two,
     16-ounce packages frozen
     unsweetened whole strawberries
1   cup packed brown sugar
1   cup water
2   lemons
3   tablespoons snipped fresh
     rosemary (optional)
     Ice cubes
1   recipe Iced Tea or one 1-liter
     bottle club soda, chilled
     Fresh strawberries (optional)

1. In a large saucepan combine fresh or frozen strawberries, brown sugar, and water. Cook and stir over medium heat until sugar dissolves.

2. Using a vegetable peeler, remove strips of peel from lemons; juice the lemons (should have ½ cup). Add strips of lemon peel, lemon juice, and rosemary to mixture in saucepan. Bring mixture just to boiling, stirring occasionally. Remove from heat. Cover; cool to room temperature.

3. Press mixture through a fine mesh sieve; discard solids (you should have about 1 quart syrup). To serve, fill glass with ice. To each glass add ½ cup Iced Tea and syrup to taste (about ½ cup). Garnish with fresh strawberries. Makes about eight (8-ounce) servings.

Nutrition facts per serving: *151 calories, 0 g total fat, 0 g saturated fat, 0 g cholesterol, 14 mg sodium, 39 g carbohydrate, 36 g total sugar, 3 g fiber, 1 g protein, 88% DV Vitamin C, 4% DV calcium, 6% DV iron.*

Strawberry Iced Tea

TEST KITCHEN TIP: SYRUP MAY
BE PREPARED, COVERED, AND
REFRIGERATED UP TO 3 DAYS.

Better
Homes
and Gardens®

Test Kitchen

Game day delight

Here's a simple meal that's perfect for watching the big game or snuggling under a blanket on the front porch.

Brew Pub Pretzels

Brew Pub Pretzels

Prep: 30 minutes   Bake: 20 minutes

- ¾ cup milk
- 4 teaspoons cooking oil
- 1 cup all-purpose flour
- 1 cup bread flour
- 2 teaspoons sugar
- ½ teaspoon salt
- 1 teaspoon active dry yeast
- 2 teaspoons salt
- 1 beaten egg white
- 1 tablespoon water
  Coarse salt or poppy seed
- 1 8-ounce package process cheese spread
- ¼ cup strong ale or beer
- ¼ teaspoon celery seed or caraway seed
  Dash pepper

1. Add milk, oil, all-purpose flour, bread flour, sugar, the ½ teaspoon salt, and yeast to a bread machine according to manufacturer's directions for a 1-pound loaf. Select dough cycle. When cycle is complete, remove dough and punch down. Turn out onto a lightly floured surface. Cover and let rest 10 minutes.

2. Roll dough into a 10×6-inch rectangle; cut into twelve ½-inch-wide strips. Gently pull each strip into a rope about 16 inches long. Shape each rope into a pretzel by crossing the rope's ends over each other, forming a circle with 4-inch tails. Twist once at the crossover point. Fold the tails over the circle. Moisten the ends and press to seal.

3. Place pretzels ½-inch apart on greased baking sheets. Bake in a 475°F. oven for 4 minutes. Remove from oven. Reduce oven temperature to 350°F.

4. Dissolve the 2 teaspoons salt in 2 quarts boiling water. Reduce heat. Gently slide pretzels, a few at a time, into simmering water. Simmer for 2 minutes, turning once. Remove with a slotted spoon; drain on a wire rack. Place ½-inch apart on a well-greased baking sheet.

5. Combine egg white and water. Brush pretzels with egg white mixture; sprinkle lightly with coarse salt or poppy seed. Bake in the 350°F. oven for 20 to 25 minutes or until golden brown. Cool slightly on wire racks.

6. Meanwhile, combine process cheese spread, ale or beer, celery seed or caraway seed, and dash pepper in a saucepan. heat and stir over medium-low heat until cheese is melted. Serve with pretzels. Makes 12 servings.

Nutrition facts per serving: *172 calories, 6 g fat, 4 g saturated fat, 13 mg cholesterol, 781 mg sodium, 19 g carbohydrate, 1 g fiber, 7 g protein.*

Chunky Steak Chili

Prep: 40 minutes   Cook: 30 minutes

- ½ pound boneless beef top round steak
- 1 15½-ounce can kidney beans
  Nonstick cooking spray
- 1 cup chopped onions (2 medium)
- 2 cloves garlic, minced
- 11 4-ounce cans low-sodium tomatoes, cut up
- 1 8-ounce can low-sodium tomato sauce
- 2 stalks celery, bias-sliced ½ inch thick
- 1 tablespoon chili powder
- 1 teaspoon brown sugar
- 1 teaspoon dried oregano, crushed
- 1 teaspoon ground cumin
  Plain non-fat yogurt or non-fat dairy sour cream (optional)
- 2 tablespoons canned chopped green chilies

1. Partially freeze beef. Trim off any fat. Thinly slice across the grain into bite-size pieces. Set aside.

2. Drain kidney beans. Rinse under cold running water. Drain off any water. Set the beans aside.

3. Coat a large saucepan with cooking spray. Add the sliced beef, onions, and garlic. Cook and stir over medium-high heat until meat is browned.

4. Stir in drained kidney beans, undrained tomatoes, tomato sauce, celery, chopped green chilies, chili powder, brown sugar, oregano, and cumin. Bring to boiling. Reduce heat. Simmer, covered, for about 30 to 40 minutes or until tender. Serve with non-fat yogurt or sour cream. Makes 4 servings.

Nutrition facts per serving: *255 calories, 3 g total fat, 1 g saturated fat, 27 mg cholesterol, 322 mg sodium, 40 g carbohydrate, 10 g fiber, 22 g protein.*

Chunky Steak Chili

Hot Chocolate by the Bowlful

Start to finish: 15 minutes

- 4 cups half-and-half, light cream, or whole milk
- 3 to 4 ounces semisweet chocolate, chopped
- 3 to 4 ounces bittersweet chocolate, chopped
- 1 tablespoon dark-colored corn syrup

Combine half-and-half, semisweet chocolate, and bittersweet chocolate in a heavy, 2-quart saucepan. Stir in dark corn syrup. Cook and stir over medium heat until chocolate melts and mixture is smooth. Serve in warmed latte bowls or mugs. Makes 8 servings.

Nutrition facts per serving: 270 calories, 23 g total fat, 14 g saturated fat, 45 mg cholesterol, 52 mg sodium, 17 g carbohydrate, 3 g fiber, 6 g protein, 2% DV Vitamin C, 12% DV calcium, 8% DV iron.

Hot Chocolate by the Bowlful

Cool-day warm-up

Just right for a cool fall day, enjoy comfort food on a smaller scale.

Mini Reubens

Mini Reubens
Start to finish: 15 minutes

30	slices party rye bread
¼	cup creamy Dijon-style mustard blend
4	ounces thinly sliced cooked corned beef
1	8-ounce can sauerkraut, rinsed, drained, and snipped
½	teaspoon caraway seed
1	cup finely shredded Swiss cheese (4 ounces)

Arrange bread slices on a baking sheet. Broil 4 to 5 inches from the heat for 1 minute on each side or until lightly toasted. Spread mustard blend lightly on one side of each bread slice. Arrange corned beef on each bread slice, cutting or folding to fit. Combine sauerkraut and caraway seed; toss until well mixed. Spoon about 1 teaspoon mixture on top of corned beef; sprinkle with about 1 teaspoon cheese. Broil 4 to 5 inches from the heat for 1 to 2 minutes or until cheese is melted. Serve at once. Makes 30.

Nutrition facts per serving: *41 calories, 2 g total fat, 1 g saturated fat, 7 mg cholesterol, 162 mg sodium, 3 g carbohydrate, 0 g fiber, 2 g protein, 2% DV Vitamin C, 3% DV calcium, 2% DV iron.*

Better Homes and Gardens®

Test Kitchen

TEST KITCHEN TIP: TO MAKE AHEAD, TOAST BREAD SLICES; COOL. SEAL TOAST IN A PLASTIC BAG AND STORE AT ROOM TEMPERATURE FOR UP TO 2 HOURS. TO SERVE: ASSEMBLE AS DIRECTED.

TEST KITCHEN TIP: YOU MAY SUBSTITUTE 4½ CUPS SHREDDED CABBAGE OR 3½ CUPS CHOPPED CAULIFLOWER FOR THE FENNEL. COOK AS DIRECTED.

Hot Fennel Cheese Dip

Prep: 25 minutes   Bake: 15 minutes
Cook: 10 minutes

4	slices bacon
3	medium fennel bulbs (8 oz. each)
2	cloves garlic, minced
1	8-ounce jar mayonnaise
1	8-ounce carton dairy sour cream
1	4-ounce package crumbled blue cheese
20	dried whole black or pink peppercorns, crushed

Finely shredded Parmesan cheese (about 2 tablespoons)
Fine dry bread crumbs (about 2 tablespoons)
Radishes and/or Belgian endive leaves

1. Preheat oven to 400°F. In a skillet cook bacon over medium heat until crisp. Remove bacon. Drain, reserving 1 tablespoon drippings in skillet. Crumble bacon; set aside.

2. To prepare fennel, cut off and discard upper stalks of fennel. Remove any wilted outer layers and cut a thin slice from the fennel base. Wash fennel and cut in half lengthwise; remove core. Cut crosswise into very thin slices.

3. Add fennel and garlic to drippings in skillet. Cook over medium heat about 10 minutes until fennel is just tender and begins to brown, stirring occasionally. Remove from heat. Add mayonnaise, sour cream, blue cheese, bacon, and peppercorns to fennel; mix well. Divide mixture between two 16-ounce oven-proof crocks, souffle dishes, or other oven-proof dishes. In a small bowl combine Parmesan cheese and bread crumbs; top mixture in each crock with Parmesan mixture.

4. Bake, uncovered, 15 minutes, or until just heated through and tops are light brown. Do not overbake. Serve with radishes and/or Belgian endive leaves. Makes 6 to 8 servings.

Nutrition facts per serving: 553 calories, 51 g total fat, 16 g saturated fat, 7 g monounsaturated fat, 18 g polyunsaturated fat, 72 mg cholesterol, 896 mg sodium, 11 g carbohydrate, 0 g total sugar, 3 g fiber, 13 g protein, 20% DV Vitamin C, 34% DV calcium, 2% DV iron.

TEST KITCHEN TIP: USE A VEGETABLE PEELER TO PEEL THE ORANGE, MAKING SURE TO GET ONLY THE OUTER PART AND AS LITTLE AS POSSIBLE OF THE BITTER WHITE LAYER UNDER THE ORANGE SKIN.

Ozark Mountain Mulled Cider

Ozark Mountain Mulled Cider

Prep: 10 minutes   Cook: 30 minutes

8	cups apple cider or apple juice
¼	cup orange juice
2	tablespoons packed brown sugar
3	inches stick cinnamon
1	tablespoon whole allspice
1	teaspoon whole cloves
1	teaspoon whole cardamom (optional)
	Peel from 1 orange
	Ground nutmeg

1. In a large saucepan, combine cider, orange juice, and sugar.

2. Wrap whole spices and orange peel in 100% cotton cheesecloth; add to saucepan. Bring to boiling; reduce heat. Cover and simmer about 30 minutes. Discard spice bag. Serve cider in mugs, sprinkled with nutmeg. Makes about 8 (7-ounce) servings.

Nutrition facts per serving: *111 calories, 0 g total fat, 0 g saturated fat, 0 mg cholesterol, 1 mg sodium, 7 g carbohydrate, 0 g fiber, 0 g protein.*

MAKE AHEAD
meals

Life on the farm is busy. There are chores to be done from sunrise to sunset, and sometimes beyond. And on top of that, there's often a job in town, plus PTA meetings, kids to drive to wrestling practice, and laundry to do. Oh, and everyone still has to eat.

With these make-ahead meals and a little planning, you can feed your family real food, even when you don't have real time. Each meal includes three make-ahead dishes, plus a store-bought item to save time.

Yes, life on the farm is busy, but all the hard work leads to great rewards. Watching newborn calves frolic in the pasture. The satisfaction that comes from a successful harvest. And making memories as meals are shared with the people you love.

Busy-morning breakfast

Get everyone off to a good start, even on the busiest days. Anyone can make cereal and toast, but why resort to that when this meal is so easy? Store-bought item: Turkey bacon or sausage.

Heart-Healthy Apple Coffee Cake

Ginger Fruit Compote

chopped apple and egg product. Stir in the ¾ cup sugar, the ¼ cup nuts, and applesauce. Add flour mixture and stir just until combined. Pour batter into prepared pan. For topping, stir together the brown sugar, the remaining all-purpose flour, whole wheat flour, and cinnamon. Cut in margarine until crumbly. Stir in remaining ¼ cup chopped nuts. Sprinkle topping over batter in pan.

3. Bake in 350°F. oven for 30 to 35 minutes or until a toothpick inserted near the center comes out clean. Cool in pan for 10 minutes. Remove from pan and serve warm. Makes 10 servings.

Make-Ahead Tip: Cool coffee cake completely. Wrap in foil and place in airtight freezer container or plastic freezer bag. Seal, label, and freeze up to 1 month. Thaw at room temperature for 2 hours. Or, reheat by placing frozen, wrapped coffee cake in 300°F. oven for 30 minutes.

Nutrition facts per serving: *203 calories, 5 g total fat, 1 g saturated fat, 0 mg cholesterol, 207 mg sodium, 37 g carbohydrate, 2 g fiber, 4 g protein.*

Heart-Healthy Apple Coffee Cake

Prep: 25 minutes   Bake: 30 minutes
Cool: 10 minutes   Stand: 10 minutes

	Nonstick cooking spray
⅔	cup all-purpose flour
½	cup whole wheat flour
1	teaspoon baking soda
1	teaspoon ground cinnamon
¼	teaspoon salt
1½	cups peeled, cored, and finely chopped apple (2 large), such as Jonathan or Granny Smith
¼	cup frozen or refrigerated egg product, thawed
¾	cup sugar
¼	cup chopped walnuts or pecans
¼	cup applesauce
1	tablespoon all-purpose flour
1	tablespoon whole wheat flour
½	teaspoon ground cinnamon
1	tablespoon margarine
¼	cup chopped walnuts or pecans
¼	cup packed brown sugar

1. Lightly coat a 9-inch round baking pan with cooking spray; set aside. In a medium bowl combine the ⅔ cup all-purpose flour, ½ cup whole wheat flour, baking soda, the 1 teaspoon cinnamon, and salt; set aside.

2. In a large mixing bowl toss together the

Ginger Fruit Compote

Prep: 25 minutes

1½	cups water
1	cup sugar
3	tablespoons lemon juice
2	tablespoons snipped crystallized ginger
8	cups assorted fruit (such as sliced kiwifruit, orange sections, chopped apple, sliced banana, and/or seedless red grapes)

1. For syrup, combine water, sugar, lemon juice, and crystallized ginger in a medium saucepan. Bring mixture to boiling; reduce heat. Cover and simmer for 5 minutes. Transfer to a bowl. Cool. Cover; chill the mixture up to 24 hours.

2. Place fruit in a large serving bowl. Pour syrup over fruit, tossing gently to coat all fruit with syrup. Cover and chill 4 to 24 hours. Makes 12 servings.

Nutrition facts per serving: *132 calories, 0 g total fat, 0 g saturated fat, 0 mg cholesterol, 3 mg sodium, 34 g carbohydrate, 2 g fiber, 1 g protein, 1% DV Vitamin A, 62% DV Vitamin C.*

TV-tray time

Let's face it ... occasionally, every family eats dinner in front of the tube, rather than at the table. Make TV-tray time terrific with this fun appetizer-inspired meal. Store-bought item: Bottled blue cheese dressing and celery sticks.

Buffalo-Style Chicken Fing

Bacon and Tomato Potato Skins

Bacon and Tomato Potato Skins
Start to finish: 45 minutes

6   large baking potatoes
2   teaspoons cooking oil
1   teaspoon chili powder
     Several dashes bottled hot pepper
     sauce
⅔   cup chopped Canadian-style bacon or
     chopped, cooked turkey bacon
1   medium tomato, finely chopped
2   tablespoons finely chopped green
     onion
4   ounces cheddar cheese or reduced-fat
     cheddar cheese, shredded (1 cup)
½   cup dairy sour cream (optional)

1. Scrub potatoes thoroughly and prick with a fork. Arrange on a microwave-safe plate. Micro-cook, uncovered, on 100 percent power (high) for 17 to 22 minutes or until almost tender, rearranging once. (Or, bake potatoes in a 425°F. oven for 40 to 45 minutes or until tender.) Cool.

2. Halve each potato lengthwise. Scoop out the inside of each potato half, leaving about a ¼-inch-thick shell. Cover and chill the leftover fluffy white part of potatoes for another use. Combine the cooking oil, chili powder, and hot pepper sauce. With a pastry brush, brush the insides of the potato halves with the oil mixture. Cut the potato halves in half lengthwise. Return to the baking sheet. Sprinkle potato quarters with bacon, tomato, and green onion. Top with cheese. To make ahead, cover and chill for up to 24 hours.

3. Bake in 450°F. oven for 10 to or until cheese is melted and pot are heated through. Serve with sour cream, if desired. Makes 24 servings.

Nutrition facts per serving: *70 calories, 2 g total fat, 1 g saturated fat, 8 mg cholesterol, 107 mg sodium, 9 g carbohydrate, 3 g protein, 2% DV Vitamin A, 13% DV Vitamin C, 3% DV calcium, 1% DV iron.*

Buffalo-Style Chicken Fingers
Prep: 25 minutes   Bake: 18 minutes

1   cup crushed corn flakes
1   tablespoon finely snipped parsley
¼   teaspoon salt
1   pound skinless, boneless chicken
     breasts
⅓   cup bottled blue cheese salad dressing
2   teaspoons water
1   to 2 teaspoons bottled hot pepper
     sauce
     Celery sticks
     Bottled blue cheese salad dressing

1. Combine crushed corn flakes, parsley, and salt in a shallow bowl or pie plate. Cut chicken breasts into strips about ¾ inch wide and 3 inches long. Combine the ⅓ cup dressing, water, and hot pepper sauce in a large mixing bowl. Add chicken; stir to coat. Roll chicken pieces individually in crumb mixture to coat. Place strips on a foil-lined baking sheet. Freeze until firm, about 2 hours.

2. To serve, heat oven to 425°F. Place frozen chicken strips in a single layer in a lightly greased 15×10×1-inch baking pan. Bake for 18 to 20 minutes or until meat is no longer pink in center and crumbs are golden. Serve warm with celery sticks and additional blue cheese dressing for dipping. Makes 12 servings.

Make-Ahead Tip: Place frozen strips in a freezer container. Cover and freeze up to 1 month.

Nutrition facts per serving: *184 calories, 12 g total fat, 2 g saturated fat, 26 mg cholesterol, 408 mg sodium, 9 g carbohydrate, 0 g fiber, 11 g protein, 2% DV Vitamin A, 6% DV Vitamin C, 3% DV calcium, 9% DV iron.*

PB&J Ice Cream Sandwiches

PB&J
Ice Cream Sandwiches

Prep: 40 minutes   Freeze: 4 to 48 hours
Bake: 8 minutes

1   **18-ounce roll refrigerated peanut butter cookie dough**
¼   **cup all-purpose flour**
6   **tablespoons preserves, such as raspberry, cherry, or strawberry)**
1   **pint vanilla bean ice cream**

1. Preheat oven to 350°F. Knead flour into cookie dough. On a lightly floured surface, roll dough into a 13½×9-inch rectangle. Cut into 1½-inch squares. Transfer to ungreased cookie sheets. Bake for 8 to 10 minutes or until edges are firm and tops are browned. Cool on cookie sheets for 1 minute. Remove and cool completely on a wire rack.

2. Place 1 teaspoon jam or preserves on flat side of 1 cookie. Place a small scoop of ice cream (about 1½ tablespoons) on jam. Top with another cookie, flat side down, and press lightly. Repeat with remaining cookies, jam, and ice cream (there will be extra cookies). Wrap and freeze 4 to 48 hours. Makes 16 sandwiches and 22 extra cookies.

Nutrition facts per serving: *175 calories, 9 g total fat, 3 g saturated fat, 4 g monounsaturated fat, 1 g polyunsaturated fat, 23 mg cholesterol, 104 mg sodium, 22 g carbohydrate, 7 g total sugar, 0 g fiber, 3 g protein, 1% DV Vitamin C, 5% DV calcium, 3% DV iron.*

Tropical twist

Make a bunch of these individual meatloaves, and they can be warmed as needed, for a hearty dinner or a yummy sandwich. Store-bought item: Canned or frozen peas.

dividual Pineapple Meatloaves

Individual Pineapple Meatloaves

Prep: 15 minutes   Bake: 30 minutes

- 1 beaten egg
- ½ cup quick-cooking rolled oats
- ½ cup finely chopped onion
- ¼ cup finely chopped green pepper
- ¼ teaspoon salt
- 1 pound lean ground beef
- 1 8-ounce can crushed pineapple (juice pack), drained
- 2 tablespoons bottled sweet-and-sour sauce or barbecue sauce (optional)

1. In a large mixing bowl stir together egg, oats, onion, green pepper, and salt. Add beef and pineapple; mix well.

2. Divide mixture into 6 equal portions. Shape each portion into a 4×2-inch loaf. Place loaves in a 13×9×2-inch baking pan.

3. Bake, uncovered, in a 350°F. oven for 30 to 35 minutes or until meat is no longer pink. Top each loaf with 1 teaspoon of the sweet-and-sour or barbecue sauce, if desired. Makes 6 servings.

Make-Ahead Tip: Prepare and shape meatloaves. Wrap in freezer paper or foil; place in airtight freezer containers or plastic freezer bags. Seal, label, and freeze up to 1 month. Thaw overnight in refrigerator and bake and serve as above.

Nutrition facts per serving: *186 calories, 8 g total fat, 99 mg cholesterol, 152 mg sodium, 10 g carbohydrate, 18 g protein.*

Tropical Fruit Cakes

Prep: 30 minutes   Chill: 2 hours
Bake: 20 minutes   Cool: 1 hour
Stand: 1 hour

1½	cups all-purpose flour
½	teaspoon baking powder
¼	teaspoon baking soda
½	cup butter
¾	cup packed brown sugar
2	eggs
¼	cup rum or pineapple juice
¼	cup pineapple juice
2	tablespoons light-colored corn syrup
1	teaspoon grated fresh ginger
1	teaspoon vanilla
1¾	cups mixed dried tropical fruit bits
½	cup chopped macadamia nuts or Brazil nuts
⅓	cup rum or pineapple juice
¼	cup rum or pineapple juice

1. Grease and lightly flour eight 1-cup fluted tube pans or six 4½×2½×1½-inch individual loaf pans. Set pans aside.

2. In a medium bowl combine flour, baking powder, and baking soda; set aside. In a large bowl beat butter with an electric mixer on medium to high speed for 30 seconds. Add brown sugar; beat until combined. Add eggs, one at a time, beating on medium speed until combined. (The batter may appear curdled.)

Combine ¼ cup rum or pineapple juice, ¼ cup pineapple juice, the corn syrup, ginger, and vanilla. Add flour mixture and rum mixture alternately to butter mixture, beating on low speed after each addition just until combined. Fold in fruit bits and nuts. Spread batter in prepared pan.

3. Bake in a 325°F. oven for 20 to 25 minutes for fluted tube pans or 30 to 35 minutes for loaf pans or until a toothpick inserted into centers comes out clean. Cool cakes in pans on wire racks for 10 minutes. Remove from pans; cool at least 1 hour on racks.

4. Poke holes in cakes using a wooden toothpick or bamboo skewer. Soak eight or six 8-inch-square pieces of double thickness 100% cotton cheesecloth with the ⅓ cup rum or pineapple juice. Wrap each cake in rum- or juice-soaked cheesecloth. Wrap each cake tightly in foil or seal in a plastic bag. Chill in refrigerator for 24 hours.

5. Remove foil or remove cakes from bags; drizzle with ¼ cup rum or pineapple juice. Rewrap with foil or return to plastic bags and refrigerate at least 24 hours. Remove cheesecloth before serving. If desired, sprinkle with sifted powdered sugar. Makes 6 or 8 cakes (24 servings).

Nutrition facts per serving: *165 calories, 7 g total fat, 3 g saturated fat, 29 mg cholesterol, 87 mg sodium, 21 g carbohydrate, 0 g fiber, 2 g protein, 4% DV Vitamin A, 1% DV Vitamin C, 2% DV calcium, 4% DV iron.*

TEST KITCHEN MAKE-AHEAD TIP: PREPARE TROPICAL FRUIT CAKES AS DIRECTED THROUGH STEP 5, EXCEPT REFRIGERATE UP TO 5 DAYS. (OR PREPARE TROPICAL FRUIT CAKES AS DIRECTED THROUGH STEP 5, EXCEPT DO NOT SPRINKLE WITH POWDERED SUGAR. PLACE IN SELF-SEALING FREEZER BAGS. SEAL, LABEL, AND FREEZE UP TO 3 MONTHS.) TO SERVE, THAW FROZEN CAKES IN FREEZER BAGS IN THE REFRIGERATOR OVERNIGHT. SERVE AS DIRECTED.

Better Homes and Gardens
Test Kitchen

Tropical Fruit Cakes

Hot start, COOL FINISH

Whether or not anyone in your family hunts, this meal will make them feel like they're enjoying a cozy dinner at the lodge. Store-bought item: Fresh or frozen fruit.

Chicken and Duck Hunter Stew

Chicken and Duck Hunter Stew
Prep: 1 hour   Cook: 45 minutes

12   chicken drumsticks (about 3 lb.), skinned, if desired
3   boneless duck breast halves, skinned and quartered*
¼   cup olive oil
3   cups assorted sliced fresh mushrooms, such as cremini, shiitake, oyster, and/or button
2   medium onions, sliced
3   cloves garlic, minced
6   medium tomatoes, seeded and chopped (about 3 cups)
3   medium green sweet peppers, cut into 1-inch pieces
1½   cups dry Marsala or beef broth
1   6-ounce can tomato paste
¾   cup pitted kalamata olives and/or green olives
2   tablespoons balsamic vinegar
1   teaspoon salt
¼   teaspoon ground black pepper
¼   cup snipped fresh oregano or marjoram
2   tablespoons snipped fresh rosemary
6   cups hot cooked Israeli couscous or couscous

1. In a 6-quart Dutch oven cook chicken drumsticks and duck, half at a time, in hot oil about 15 minutes or until lightly browned, turning to brown evenly. Remove chicken and duck, reserving drippings in the Dutch oven; set drumsticks aside. Cover and chill the duck portions in the refrigerator.

2. Add mushrooms, onions, and garlic to drippings in pot. Cook and stir about 5 minutes or until vegetables are just tender. Return drumsticks to Dutch oven.

3. Meanwhile, in a large bowl, combine tomatoes, sweet peppers, Marsala, tomato paste, olives, vinegar, salt, and black pepper. Pour over drumsticks in pot. Bring to boiling; reduce heat. Simmer, covered, for 20 minutes. Add duck; return to boiling. Reduce heat and simmer 25 to 30 minutes more or until poultry is tender. Just before serving, stir in oregano and rosemary. Serve stew with couscous. Makes 12 servings.

Make-Ahead Tip: Prepare stew as above, adding herbs before freezing, if desired. Chill the stew quickly by placing the Dutch oven in a sink of ice water. Divide mixture between two 2½- to 3-quart freezer containers. Seal, label, and freeze up to 1 month. To reheat, place freezer containers in refrigerator overnight to partially thaw. Place mixture in Dutch oven.

Cook over medium-low heat until mixture is completely thawed. Increase heat to medium and cook just until bubbly, about 35 to 40 minutes total (do not overcook or duck may toughen). Add herbs just before serving if not added before freezing.

*NOTE: TO MAKE THIS STEW WITH ALL CHICKEN: SUBSTITUTE 12 CHICKEN THIGHS FOR THE DUCK; ADD THE THIGHS AND DRUMSTICKS BACK INTO THE POT ALL AT ONCE.

Nutrition facts per serving: *393 calories, 14 g total fat, 3 g saturated fat, 6 g monounsaturated fat, 2 g polyunsaturated fat, 129 mg cholesterol, 407 mg sodium, 28 g carbohydrate, 5 g total sugar, 3 g fiber, 33 g protein, 62% Vitamin C, 4% DV calcium, 22% DV iron.*

Decadent French Silk Pie
Traditional French silk pie is made with uncooked eggs. Because we wanted to enjoy this ultra-rich dessert without worry, we reworked our recipe to completely cook the egg yolks. It's still every bit as decadent as the classic.
Prep: 40 minutes   Chill: 5 to 24 hours

1   baked pastry shell
1   cup whipping cream
1   cup semisweet chocolate pieces (6 ounces)
⅓   cup butter
⅓   cup sugar
2   egg yolks, beaten
3   tablespoons crème de cacao or whipping cream
½   cup whipping cream, whipped
1   recipe Double-Chocolate Curls

1. Prepare baked pastry shell; set aside. In a heavy, medium saucepan, combine the 1 cup whipping cream, the chocolate pieces, butter, and sugar. Cook over low heat, stirring constantly, until chocolate is melted (about 10 minutes). Remove from heat.

2. Gradually stir half of the hot mixture into egg yolks. Return egg yolk mixture to chocolate mixture in saucepan. Cook over medium-low heat, stirring constantly, until mixture is slightly thickened and begins to bubble (about 5 minutes). Remove from heat. (Mixture may appear to separate.) Stir in the crème de cacao. Place saucepan in a bowl of ice water; stir occasionally until the mixture stiffens and becomes hard to stir (about 20 minutes).

3. Transfer cooled mixture to a medium mixing bowl. Beat with an electric mixer on medium to high speed for 2 to 3 minutes or until light and fluffy. Spread in the cooled pastry shell. Cover and chill for at least 5 hours or up to 24 hours. To serve, top with whipped cream. If desired, garnish with Double-Chocolate Curls. Serves 8.

Double-Chocolate Curls: Line a 4 ½ × 2 ½ × 2-inch or 6 × 3 × 2-inch loaf pan with heavy foil; set aside. Melt 3 ounces semisweet chocolate and 3 ounces white chocolate separately according to package directions. Spread half of the semisweet chocolate in prepared pan. Drizzle with half of the white chocolate. With a spatula, carefully smooth white chocolate over semisweet chocolate layer in pan. Repeat layers with remaining semisweet chocolate and white chocolate, carefully smoothing each layer. Cover and let stand at room temperature for 3 to 4 hours or until completely set. (The white chocolate may set up more quickly than the semisweet chocolate.) When chocolate is set, grasp foil and remove block from pan. Pull back foil to expose one side of the block. Run a vegetable peeler over the side of the block. To store the block, wrap in foil and place in an airtight container. Store in the refrigerator for up to 1 month or in the freezer for up to 3 months. Bring chocolate to room temperature before making curls.

Nutrition facts per serving: *533 calories, 41 g total fat, 21 g saturated fat, 137 mg cholesterol, 168 mg sodium, 31 g carbohydrate, 3 g fiber, 4 g protein.*

TEST KITCHEN TIP: TIP: BE SURE TO USE REAL SEMISWEET CHOCOLATE PIECES. DO NOT SUBSTITUTE PRODUCTS LABELED IMITATION CHOCOLATE PIECES OR CHOCOLATE-FLAVORED.

STATE FAIR *food*

For generations, farmers have set aside their tools for a day or two to take their families to the state fair. Once, it was common for farm wives to pack a lunch for the family, then they'd head back to the car at lunchtime, find a shady spot, and eat together.

Today, it's more common – albeit expensive – to eat at one of the producer tents or choose something from the many vendors. And, of course, many of those foods will be fried and served on a stick.

The fair comes only once a year, but that doesn't mean you can't enjoy fair food anytime – in moderation, of course! Here are some fair favorites, along with a number of Successful Farming® recipe contest winners from the Iowa State Fair.

117

food
big taste,
BIG FUN

Grilled Behemoth Drum

People stand in line for hours for these drumsticks at the Iowa State Fair. And the gentleman who entered this potato bread in a baking contest at the Ohio State Fair said he loves the red tint because it's just like his wife's hair. Give that man a blue ribbon!

Grilled Behemoth Drumsticks

Prep: 5 minutes (20 minutes to preheat grill)
Grill: 45 minutes

4   ¾- to 1-pound turkey drumsticks
1   tablespoon cooking oil
    Salt
    Pepper

1. Brush drumsticks with cooking oil. Sprinkle with salt and pepper.
2. In a covered grill, arrange preheated coals around a drip pan. Test for medium heat above pan. Place the drumsticks on grill above the pan (not directly over coals).
3. Lower grill hood and grill for 45 minutes to 1 hour or until tender but no longer pink, turning once. Add coals to maintain heat as necessary. (For a gas grill, preheat grill. Reduce heat to medium. Adjust for indirect cooking. Place the turkey on grill rack, not directly over the heat. Grill as above.) Makes 4 servings.

Nutrition facts per serving: *233 calories, 10 g total fat, 83 mg cholesterol, 120 mg sodium, 0 g carbohydrate.*

My Fair Ladies Potato Bread

Prep: 25 minutes   Rise: 1 hour 20 minutes
Bake: 35 minutes

¾   cup buttermilk or sour milk
¾   cup packaged instant mashed potato flakes or buds
⅔   cup tomato juice
¼   cup butter, cut up
1   tablespoon sugar
1   teaspoon salt
¼   teaspoon ground white pepper
1   package active dry yeast
2   to 2¼ cups bread flour or all-purpose flour
⅓   cup dark or medium rye flour

1. In a large bowl, combine buttermilk or sour milk and potato flakes; set aside.
2. In a small saucepan, heat and stir tomato juice, butter, sugar, salt, and white pepper until warm (120°F. to 130°F.) and butter almost melts, stir into buttermilk mixture. (Mixture may appear lumpy.)
3. Stir in yeast. Add 1 cup bread or all-purpose flour; beat with an electric mixer on low speed for 30 seconds, scraping side of bowl. Beat on high speed for 3 minutes. Stir in rye flour and as much of the remaining bread flour as you can with a spoon. Turn dough onto a lightly floured surface.
4. Knead in enough remaining bread flour to make moderately stiff dough that is smooth and elastic (6 to 8 minutes total). Shape dough into ball. Place in lightly greased bowl, turning once to grease surface of dough. Cover; let dough rise in a warm place until double in size (50 to 60 minutes).
5. Grease a cookie sheet; set aside. Punch dough down; cover and let rest 10 minutes. Shape into a ball; place on prepared cookie sheet. Flatten to a circle 6 inches in diameter. Cover; let rise until nearly double in size (30 to 40 minutes).
6. Bake in a 350°F. oven for 35 to 40 minutes or until bread sounds hollow when lightly tapped. Remove from baking sheet; cool on wire rack. Makes 1 loaf (16 servings).

Nutrition facts per serving: *115 calories, 4 g total fat, 2 g saturated fat, 9 mg cholesterol, 228 mg sodium, 18 g carbohydrate, 1 g fiber, 3 g protein.*

Better Homes and Gardens
Test Kitchen

TEST KITCHEN TIP: TO TEST FOR MEDIUM HEAT, YOU SHOULD BE ABLE TO HOLD YOUR HAND OVER THE HEAT AT THE HEIGHT OF THE FOOD FOR 4 SECONDS BEFORE YOU HAVE TO PULL AWAY.

Better Homes and Gardens
Test Kitchen

TEST KITCHEN TIP: TO MAKE ¾ CUP SOUR MILK, PLACE 2 TEASPOONS LEMON JUICE OR VINEGAR IN A GLASS MEASURING CUP. ADD ENOUGH MILK TO MAKE ¾ CUP LIQUID; STIR. LET STAND FOR 5 MINUTES BEFORE USING.

North 40 Berry Pie

Farm-Fresh Ice Cream

Prep: 40 minutes   Chill: 4 hours
Freeze: 25 minutes

3	cups milk
1½	cups sugar
1	teaspoon salt
8	egg yolks, beaten
3	cups whipping cream
1	tablespoon vanilla

1. In a large saucepan combine milk, sugar, and salt; stir in egg yolks. Cook and stir over medium heat just until mixture comes to a boil.

2. Quickly cool the custard by placing the saucepan into a sink full of ice water for 1 to 2 minutes, stirring constantly.

3. Pour custard mixture into a bowl. Cover surface with plastic wrap. Chill 4 to 24 hours.

4. Stir whipping cream and vanilla into chilled custard.

5. Freeze ice cream mixture in 4- or 5-quart ice cream freezer according to manufacturer's directions. Hold for 4 hours. Makes 2 quarts.

Nutrition facts per ½-cup serving: 277 calories, 20 g total fat, 12 g saturated fat, 168 mg cholesterol, 188 mg sodium, 22 g carbohydrate, 0 g fiber, 4 g protein, 17% DV Vitamin A, 1% DV Vitamin C, 9% DV calcium, 2% DV iron.

North 40 Berry Pie

Prep: 30 minutes   Bake: 45 minutes

2	cups all-purpose flour
1	teaspoon salt
¾	cup shortening
1	egg
3	tablespoons water
1	teaspoon cider vinegar
1⅓	cups sugar
2	tablespoons quick-cooking tapioca
4½	teaspoons cornstarch
2	cups blackberries
2	cups red raspberries
1	tablespoon lemon juice
2	tablespoons butter, cut up
	Milk
	Sugar

1. In a medium mixing bowl stir together flour and salt.

2. Using a pastry blender, cut in shortening until pieces are pea size.

3. Combine egg, water and vinegar. Add 1 tablespoon at a time to flour mixture; gently toss with a fork. Push moistened dough to the side of the bowl. Repeat until all the flour mixture is moistened. If necessary, add a little more water.

4. Divide the dough in half and form each half into a ball. On a lightly floured surface, roll one dough ball to a 12-inch circle. Transfer pastry to 9-inch pie plate and ease pastry into pie plate without stretching it; set aside. Roll remaining dough to a 12-inch circle; cover and set aside.

5. In a large bowl stir together the 1½ cups sugar, the tapioca, and cornstarch. Stir in all of the berries and the lemon juice. Transfer to pastry-lined pie plate.

6. Trim pastry to ½ inch beyond rim of dish, reserving trimmings. Dot with butter. Cut remaining pastry into ½-inch wide strips. Weave strips over filling in a lattice pattern. Press ends of strips into bottom pastry rim. Fold bottom pastry over strip ends; seal and crimp edge as desired.

7. Roll reserved trimmings to ¼-inch thick; cut with small star cutters; brush star bottoms lightly with milk and attach to crust in a decorative pattern.

8. Brush pastry with milk and sprinkle with additional sugar. Cover edges of pie with foil. Bake in a 375°F. oven for 25 minutes; remove foil and bake 20 to 25 minutes more or until pastry is golden and filling is bubbly. Cool on wire rack. Makes 8 servings.

Nutrition facts per serving: 480 calories, 23 g total fat, 7 g saturated fat, 35 mg cholesterol, 323 mg sodium, 64 g carbohydrate, 5 g fiber, 5 g protein, 5% DV Vitamin A, 25% DV Vitamin C, 3% DV calcium, 11% DV iron.

food

fair food
ON A STICK

It's not official fair food unless it's served on a stick. You'll need more than two hands to carry all these treats, including the chocolatey waffles made famous at the Minnesota State Fair.

Corn Dogs with a Kick
Start to finish: 30 minutes

1	cup all-purpose flour
⅔	cup yellow cornmeal
2	tablespoons sugar
1½	teaspoons baking powder
½	teaspoon dry mustard
¼	teaspoon salt
2	tablespoons shortening
1	beaten egg
¾	cup milk
8	to 10 wooden skewers (look for them at craft shops)
1	pound frankfurters, smoked frankfurters, or cheese-filled

frankfurters (8 to 10)
Cooking oil
Catsup (optional)
Mustard (optional)

1. In a bowl, stir together flour, cornmeal, sugar, baking powder, dry mustard, and salt. Cut in shortening until mixture resembles fine crumbs.

2. In a bowl, mix together egg and milk. Add to flour mixture and mix well.

3. Insert wooden skewers into the ends of frankfurters. Pour cooking oil into skillet to a depth of 1 inch; heat oil to 365°F.

4. Coat franks with batter. (If batter is too thick, add 1 to 2 tablespoons milk.) Place coated franks, 3 at a time, in hot oil. Turn franks with tongs after 10 seconds to prevent batter from sliding off. Cook for 2 to 3 minutes more or until golden, turning again halfway through cooking time.

5. Serve hot with catsup and mustard, if you like. Makes 8 to 10 servings.

Nutrition facts per serving: *367 calories, 28 g total fat, 46 mg cholesterol, 632 mg sodium, 21 g carbohydrate.*

Corn Dogs with a Kick

STATE FAIR
food

Choose-a-Flavor Caramel Apples
Prep: 25 minutes

- 10 small apples (Jonathans work well)
- 10 wooden sticks
- 1 cup coarsely chopped peanuts, crushed pretzels, or crunchy granola (optional)
- 21 ounces (about 75) vanilla caramels, unwrapped
- 3 tablespoons water
- 6 drops cinnamon oil or 1 cup semisweet chocolate pieces, or ½ cup creamy peanut butter

1. Wash and dry apples. Remove stems. Insert 1 wooden stick into the stem end of each apple. Place apples on a buttered baking sheet. Place chopped nuts, pretzels, or granola in a shallow dish, if using; set aside.

2. In a heavy medium saucepan heat and stir the caramels and water over medium-low heat just until caramels are melted. Remove saucepan from heat. Stir in cinnamon oil, chocolate pieces or peanut butter.

3. Working quickly, dip each apple into hot caramel mixture, spooning caramel evenly over apple. (If necessary, add hot water, 1 teaspoon at a time, to caramel mixture to make of dipping consistency.) To remove excess caramel, scrape off bottom of apple with a metal spatula. If desired, dip bottoms into peanuts, pretzels, or granola. Set apples on prepared baking sheet and let stand about 30 minutes or until firm. Makes 10 dipped apples.

Nutrition facts per serving: 384 calories, 11 g total fat, 6 g saturated fat, 0 mg cholesterol, 156 mg sodium, 67 g carbohydrate, 7 g fiber, 2 g protein, 9% DV Vitamin C, 10% DV calcium, 6% DV iron.

Choose-a-Flavor Caramel Apples

Minnesota Fudge Puppies
Prep: 20 minutes

1 cup semisweet chocolate pieces (6 ounces)
1 cup milk chocolate pieces (6 ounces)
2 teaspoons shortening
5 frozen buttermilk waffles or Belgian waffles
  Almond brickle pieces, colorful sprinkles, toasted coconut, or other crunchy toppings
  Whipped cream (optional)

1. In a small saucepan, melt semisweet chocolate, milk chocolate, and shortening over low heat, stirring constantly.

2. Meanwhile, place waffles in a single layer on an ungreased baking sheet; toast in the oven according to package directions. Halve each waffle crosswise.

3. Dip waffles in chocolate or spoon chocolate over waffles to coat. Remove from chocolate with a fork, allowing excess chocolate to flow back into pan.

4. Insert a wooden skewer or ice cream stick into each waffle half. Place on a waxed-paper-lined baking sheet. Sprinkle with topping. Refrigerate for 30 minutes or until chocolate is set.

5. Serve fudge puppies topped with whipped cream, if you like. Makes 10.

Nutrition facts per serving: *240 calories, 14 g total fat, 1 mg cholesterol, 161 mg sodium, 30 g carbohydrate.*

Lemon-Orange Shakeups
Start to finish: 5 minutes

½ of a lemon
½ of an orange*
3 tablespoons sugar
  Ice cubes (about 1¼ cups)
  Water (about 3 tablespoons)
  Orange wedges or lemon slices (optional)

1. In a 16-ounce shaker, squeeze juice from the lemon and orange halves. Add sugar.

2. Add enough ice cubes to fill two-thirds full. Add water to cover ice.

3. Cover and shake. Serve in a tall glass. Garnish with orange wedges or lemon slices, if you like. Makes 1 serving.

*Note: For a lemon-only shakeup, substitute ½ of a lemon for the orange half.

Nutrition facts per serving: *173 calories, 0 g total fat, 0 mg cholesterol, 3 mg sodium, 45 g carbohydrate.*

STATE FAIR food farmer's FAVORITE

Pork chops on a stick have exploded in popularity over the past few years. It's about time someone came up with a way to eat a pork chop while walking around the fair!

Pork Chops on a Stick
Prep: 15 minutes   Marinate: 1 hour
Cook: Fry 6 minutes per batch

- 8   6-ounce boneless pork loin chops, about 1 inch thick
- ½   cup bottled Italian salad dressing
       Peanut oil
- 8   8×¼-inch-thick wooden skewers or dowels
       Honey mustard or bottled barbecue sauce

1. Place chops in a resealable plastic bag set in a shallow dish. Pour salad dressing over chops; seal bag. Marinate in the refrigerator for 1 hour, turning bag occasionally.

2. Meanwhile, preheat oil to 350°F. Drain chops, discarding marinade. Insert a wooden skewer into a short side of each chop. Fry the chops, half at a time, for 5 to 8 minutes or until 160°F. (To test for doneness, carefully remove one chop from the hot oil. Insert an instant-read thermometer into side of chop.) Be cautious of splattering oil. Maintain oil temperature around 350°F. Remove chops from hot oil and drain on wire racks. Serve chops with honey mustard. Makes 8 chops.

Nutrition facts per serving: *344 calories, 19 g total fat, saturated fat, 8 g monounsaturated fat, 93 mg cholesterol, 243 sodium, 3 g carbohydrate, 0 g fiber, 37 g protein, 1% DV Vitamin C, 1% DV calcium, 8% DV iron.*

Pork Chops on a Stick

Best Homemade French Fries

Prep: 20 minutes

Cook: 7 minutes per batch

1½ **pounds russet or baking potatoes**
   Peanut oil for deep-fat frying
   Sea salt or kosher salt or salt

1. Peel the potatoes, if desired, and cut length-wise into ¼- to ⅜-inch sticks. Soak in ice water if not ready to fry.

2. In a deep-fat fryer, heat peanut oil according to manufacturer's directions to 365°F., or heat oil in a 3-quart or larger saucepan to 365°F. (saucepan should be no more than half full).

3. Drain the potatoes well. Pat potatoes thoroughly dry on paper toweling. Fry the potatoes, about one-third at a time, until potatoes are tender in the center and edges are just beginning to color and blister, about 7 to 9 minutes. Remove with a frying basket and drain on paper toweling.

4. To serve, sprinkle lightly with salt. Makes 4 servings.

Nutrition facts per serving: *220 calories, 14 g total fat, 2 g saturated fat, 6 g monounsaturated fat, 4 g polyunsaturated fat, 0 mg cholesterol, 408 mg sodium, 23 g carbohydrate, 2 g total sugar, 2 g fiber, 3 g protein, 32% DV Vitamin C, 1% DV calcium, 5% DV iron.*

est Homemade French Fries

Blueberry Grunt

- 2 cups fresh or frozen blueberries
- ½ cup sugar
- 1 tablespoon lemon juice
- ½ teaspoon ground cinnamon
- ¼ teaspoon ground nutmeg
- ¾ cup all-purpose flour
- 2 tablespoons sugar
- 1 teaspoon baking powder
- ¼ cup butter
- ¼ cup milk
  Light cream, half-and-half or milk

1. In a 3-quart saucepan combine blueberries, ½ cup sugar, lemon juice, cinnamon, nutmeg and 1 cup water. Bring to boiling, reduce heat. Cover and simmer 5 minutes.

2. Meanwhile, for dumplings, in a medium mixing bowl combine the flour, 2 tablespoons sugar, and baking powder. Cut in the butter till mixture resembles coarse crumbs. Add ¼ cup of milk; stir just till moistened.

3. Drop dumplings by tablespoons to make 6 mounds atop bubbling blueberry mixture. Cover and simmer 15 minutes (do not lift cover).

4. For each serving, spoon 1 dumpling and some of the blueberry mixture into a dessert bowl. Serve warm with light cream, half-and-half or milk. Makes 6 servings.

Nutrition facts per serving: *276 calories, 12 g total fat, 4 g saturated fat, 22 mg cholesterol, 151 mg sodium, 41 g carbohydrate, 2 g fiber, 3 g protein, 12% DV Vitamin A, 13% DV Vitamin C, 9% DV calcium, 6% DV iron.*

Blueberry Grunt

blue-ribbon FAIR MEAL

Bun-busting tenderloins are a must-have treat at the fair,

and nothing says summer like corn on the cob.

Pork Tenderloin Sandwiches

Start to finish: 25 minutes

¾ **pound pork tenderloin**
¼ **cup all-purpose flour**
¼ **teaspoon onion powder or garlic powder**
¼ **teaspoon pepper**
1 **beaten egg**
1 **tablespoon milk or water**
1 **cup finely crushed rich round crackers (about 24) or ¾ cup fine dry bread crumbs**
1 **tablespoon cooking oil**
4 **hamburger buns or kaiser rolls, split and toasted
    Mustard, catsup, onion slices, dill pickle slices, and/or roasted red sweet peppers (optional)**

1. Cut pork crosswise into 4 slices. With a meat mallet, pound each pork slice between plastic wrap to ¼-inch thickness.

2. In a shallow bowl combine flour, onion or garlic powder, and pepper. In another shallow bowl combine egg and milk or water. In a third bowl place crushed crackers or bread crumbs. Dip each pork slice into the flour mixture, coating well, then into the egg mixture, and then into the crumbs to coat.

3. In a large skillet cook two pork slices in hot oil over medium heat for 6 to 8 minutes or until pork is done, turning once. (Or cook on a well-greased griddle.) Remove from skillet; keep warm. Repeat with remaining slices, adding more oil, if necessary.

4. Place on buns. If desired, serve with mustard, catsup, onion, pickle, and/or peppers. Makes 4 servings.

Nutrition facts per serving: *405 calories, 15 g total fat, 4 g saturated fat, 114 mg cholesterol, 477 mg sodium, 40 g carbohydrate, 26 g protein.*

Pork Tenderloin Sandwich

Grilled Corn on the Cob with Herbs

Grilled Corn on the Cob with Herbs
Prep: 20 minutes   Grill: 25 minutes

6	fresh ears yellow and/or white sweet corn (with husks)
6	tablespoons butter or margarine, softened
36	sprigs or leaves of cilantro or basil
	100% cotton kitchen string
	Lime or lemon juice (optional)

1. Gently rinse corn. Pat dry. Spread softened butter or margarine evenly over each ear of corn. Space 6 herb sprigs or leaves evenly around cob, gently pressing herbs into butter. Carefully fold husks back around tops of cobs. Tie husk tops with kitchen string.

2. Grill corn on the rack of a covered grill directly over medium coals for 25 to 30 minutes, until kernels are tender, turning and rearranging with long-handled tongs three times. Or, grill corn indirectly on the rack of a covered grill, arranging coals around the edge of the grill. Place corn on the rack above the cneter of the grill, and cook 25 to 30 minutes, until kernels are tender, turning and rearranging three times.

3. To serve, remove the string from corn. Peel back husks. If desired, squeeze lime juice over cilantro corn or lemon juice over basil corn. Makes 6 servings.

Nutrition facts per serving: *185 calories, 13 g total fat, 8 g saturated fat, 33 mg cholesterol, 137 mg sodium, 17 g carbohydrate, 2 g fiber, 3 g protein, 14% DV Vitamin A, 9% DV Vitamin C, 1% DV calcium, 3% DV iron.*

Farm-Fresh Strawberry Ice Cream
Prep: 20 minutes   Stand: 4 hours
Chill: 4 hours   Freeze: 20 minutes

8	egg yolks, lightly beaten
2	cups milk
1½	cups sugar
¼	teaspoon salt
3	cups whipping cream
2	cups strawberry-flavored carbonated beverage, chilled
3	cups fresh strawberries, hulled and finely chopped

1. In a heavy medium saucepan combine egg yolks, milk, sugar, and salt. Cook, stirring over medium heat until mixture is thickened (about 10 to 12 minutes). Remove from heat. Transfer to a medium bowl. Cover surface of custard mixture with plastic wrap. Chill 4 hours or overnight until completely chilled. (Or, to chill quickly, place the bowl in a larger bowl of ice water, cover loosely, and stir occasionally for 1 hour.)

2. Stir together custard, whipping cream, carbonated strawberry beverage, and fresh strawberries. Freeze ice cream mixture in a 4- to 5-quart ice cream freezer according to manufacturer's directions. Ripen 4 hours (mixture will be slightly soft after ripening). Transfer to a freezer container and store in freezer. Makes about 2½ quarts (twenty ½-cup servings).

Nutrition facts per serving: *231 calories, 16 g total fat, 133 mg cholesterol, 59 mg sodium, 21 g carbohydrate, 0 g fiber, 3 g protein.*

Mom's Angel Food Cake

Prep: 50 minutes   Bake: 40 minutes

12	egg whites
1¼	cups sifted cake flour
½	cup sugar
1½	teaspoons cream of tartar
1	teaspoon vanilla
¼	teaspoon salt
¼	teaspoon almond extract
1⅓	cups sugar
	Fresh berries (optional)
	Sweetened whipped cream (optional)

1. Preheat oven to 350°F. In a very large mixing bowl allow the egg whites to stand at room temperature for about 30 minutes.

2. Meanwhile, sift flour and ½ cup sugar together 3 times; set aside.

3. Add cream of tartar, vanilla, salt, and almond extract to egg whites. Beat with an electric mixer on medium speed until soft peaks form (tips curl).

4. Gradually add the 1⅓ cups sugar, about 2 tablespoons at a time, beating on high until stiff peaks form (tips stand straight).

5. Sift about one-fourth of the flour mixture over beaten egg whites; fold in gently. (If bowl is too full, transfer to a larger bowl.)

6. Repeat, folding in remaining flour mixture by fourths.

7. Spoon into an ungreased 10-inch tube pan. Gently cut through batter with a thin metal spatula to remove any large air pockets.

8. Bake on the lowest rack of oven for 40 to 45 minutes or until the tops springs back when lightly touched. Immediately invert cake (leave in pan) and cool thoroughly. Loosen sides of cake from pan with a long thin knife; remove cake.

9. If desired, serve cake with fresh berries and sweetened whipped cream. Makes 12 servings.

Nutrition facts per serving: *174 calories, 0 g total fat, 0 mg cholesterol, 104 mg sodium, 39 g carbohydrate, 0 g fiber, 5 g protein, 5% DV iron.*

Mom's Angel Food Cake

state fair
classic

Spicy Italian Grinder

You may be at a fair in the Midwest, but that doesn't mean you can't enjoy the taste of Italy. These grinders are too good to pass up!

Spicy Italian Grinder
Prep: 20 minutes   Cook: 15 minutes

1	16-ounce loaf unsliced Italian or French bread (about 16×4 inches) or 6 individual French rolls
1	pound extra-lean ground pork or beef
1	cup sliced fresh mushrooms
¾	cup chopped onion
½	cup chopped green sweet pepper
1	garlic clove, minced
1	or 2 dried red chili peppers, crushed
1	teaspoon paprika
½	teaspoon dried thyme, crushed
½	teaspoon fennel seed, crushed
¼	teaspoon salt
⅛	teaspoon ground black pepper
1	8-ounce can low-sodium tomato sauce*
2	tablespoons grated Parmesan cheese
¾	cup shredded reduced-fat mozzarella cheese (3 ounces)

1. Split bread loaf in half horizontally. Hollow out bottom half of the loaf, leaving about 1-inch shell. (If using individual rolls, hollow them out slightly.) Set aside. (Reserve the bread pieces from inside of the loaf for another use, such as bread crumbs.)

2. In a large skillet cook pork or beef, mushrooms, onion, sweet pepper, and garlic until no pink remains in pork. Drain well. Stir in the red chili peppers, paprika, thyme, fennel seed, salt, and black pepper. Stir in the tomato sauce. Heat to boiling; reduce heat. Cover and simmer for 10 minutes. Stir in Parmesan cheese.

3. Spoon meat mixture into the bottom half of the bread loaf or rolls. Sprinkle mozzarella cheese over the meat mixture; cover with loaf or roll top(s). Place sandwich in a shallow baking pan or on a baking sheet. Cover tightly with foil and bake in a 375°F. oven for 15 to 20 minutes or until cheese melts and sandwich is hot. (For smaller sandwiches, wrap each in foil and place on a baking sheet or in a shallow baking pan. Bake in a 300°F. oven for 10 minutes to warm.)

4. To serve the large sandwich, use a serrated knife to slice the loaf crosswise into 6 portions. Makes 6 main-dish servings.

*Note: By using this low-sodium product instead of regular tomato sauce, you reduce the sodium in an individual serving by about 225 milligrams.

Nutrition facts per serving: *410 calories, 13 g total fat, 5 g saturated fat, 59 mg cholesterol, 724 mg sodium, 45 g carbohydrate, 1 g fiber, 26 g protein.*

food

Italian Doughnuts

- 1   15-ounce container ricotta cheese
- 4   eggs
- 1   tablespoon vanilla
- 1½ cups all-purpose flour
- ½   cup granulated sugar
- 2   tablespoons baking powder
- ½   teaspoon salt
  Cooking oil for frying
  Sifted powdered sugar
  or granulated sugar or
  cinnamon/sugar

1. In a large bowl beat ricotta cheese with an electric mixer on medium speed until smooth. Add eggs and vanilla; beat until com- bined. Add flour, granulated sugar, bak- ing powder, and salt. Beat on low speed until just combined. Let batter stand for 30 minutes.

2. Drop batter by well-rounded teaspoonfuls, four or five at a time, into deep hot fat (365°F.). Cook 2½ to 3 minutes or until golden brown, turning once. Remove doughnuts with slotted spoon and drain on paper towels. Repeat with remaining batter. Cool completely. Shake doughnuts in a bag with powdered sugar, granulated sugar, or cinnamon/ sugar mixture. Makes 3 dozen.

Nutrition facts per serving: *102 calories, 6 g total fat, 2 g saturated fat, 30 mg cholesterol, 107 mg sodium, 9 g carbohydrate, 0 g fiber, 3 g protein, 7% DV calcium, 2% DV iron.*

Italian Doughnut

Strawberry Italian Ice

Prep: 25 minutes
Freeze: 6 hours or overnight

1	cup sugar
¾	cup water
1	tablespoon finely shredded orange peel
2	teaspoons finely shredded lemon peel
1½	teaspoons finely shredded lime peel
⅓	cup orange juice
3	tablespoons lemon juice
2	tablespoons lime juice
4	cups sliced fresh strawberries

1. In a medium saucepan combine sugar, water, and peels. Bring to boiling; reduce heat. Simmer, uncovered, 5 minutes. Cool slightly. Strain and discard peels. Stir in orange, lemon, and lime juices.

2. In a blender container or food processor bowl combine half of the juice mixture and half of the strawberries. Cover and blend or process with several on/off turns or until nearly smooth (leave some small chunks of strawberries). Transfer to a 2-quart freezer container. Repeat with remaining juice mixture and strawberries. Cover and freeze 6 hours or overnight, stirring once after freezing for 3 hours.

3. To serve, scrape across frozen mixture with a large spoon and place into individual serving dishes (if mixture is too firm, let stand at room temperature 20 to 30 minutes). Makes 8 servings.

Nutrition facts per serving: *123 calories, 0 g total fat, 0 mg cholesterol, 2 mg sodium, 31 g carbohydrate, 29 g total sugar, 2 g fiber, 1 g protein, 86% DV Vitamin C, 2% DV calcium, 2% DV iron.*

Dad's Gooseberry Pie
Prep: 35 minutes   Bake 60 minutes

1   recipe Country Tearoom Pastry
3   15-ounce cans gooseberries, drained
1   cup sugar
¼   cup all-purpose flour
¼   teaspoon ground cinnamon
⅛   teaspoon salt
1   tablespoon butter

1. Preheat oven to 375°F. Prepare Country Tearoom Pastry.

2. On a lightly floured surface, use your hands to slightly flatten 1 dough ball. Roll dough from center of edges into a circle 12 inches in diameter. To transfer pastry, wrap it around the rolling pin; unroll into a 9-inch pie plate without stretching it; set aside.

3. For filling, in a large bowl stir together gooseberries, sugar, flour, cinnamon and salt (filling will be wet). Pour filling into pastry-lined pie plate. Dot with butter. Trim pastry even with rim of pie plate.

4. Roll remaining dough ball into a circle about 12 inches in diameter. Cut slits to allow steam to escape. Place pastry on filling; trim to ½ inch beyond the edge of the pie plate. Fold top pastry under bottom pastry. Crimp edge as desired.

5. Bake for 60 to 65 minutes or until pastry is golden and filling is bubbly. Cool on wire rack. (Filling will be slightly soft.) Makes 8 servings.

Country Tearoom Pastry: In a large bowl stir together 2 cups all-purpose flour, 1½ teaspoons sugar, and ¾ teaspoon salt. Using a pastry blender, cut in ½ cup lard or shortening until pieces are pea size. In a small bowl stir together 1 egg yolk, 1 tablespoon cider vinegar, and ⅓ cup ice water. Add to flour mixture. Stir wth fork until all is moistened. If necessary, add ice water 1 tablespoon at a time to moisten. Using your hands, knead gently until mixture forms a ball. Divide in half.

Nutrition facts per serving: *463 calories, 15 g total fat, 41 mg cholesterol, 280 mg sodium, 80 g carbohydrate, 5 g fiber, 5 g protein.*

Dad's Gooseberry Pie

Caramel Corn

Prep: 20 minutes   Bake: 20 minutes

      Nonstick spray coating
   8 **cups popped popcorn (about
      ⅓ to ½ cup unpopped)**
  ¾ **cup packed brown sugar**
  ⅓ **cup butter (no substitutes)**
   3 **tablespoons light-color corn
      syrup**
  ¼ **teaspoon baking soda**
  ¼ **teaspoon vanilla**

1. Spray an 18×12×2-inch baking pan with nonstick spray. Remove unpopped kernels from popped corn. Place popcorn in pan; keep warm in a 300°F. oven.

2. Butter sides of heavy 1½-quart saucepan. Add brown sugar, butter, and corn syrup. Clip candy thermometer to side of pan. Cook and stir over medium heat to 255°F., hard-ball stage (about 4 minutes). Remove saucepan from heat. Stir in baking soda and vanilla; pour over popcorn. Stir gently to coat.

3. Bake in a 300°F. oven for 15 minutes. Stir and bake 5 minutes more. Remove from oven; spread onto a large piece of foil and cool completely. Break into clusters. Makes 9 cups.

  Nutrition facts per serving: *171 calories, 7 g total fat, 4 g saturated fat, 18 mg cholesterol, 113 mg sodium, 27 g carbohydrate, 1 g fiber, 1 g protein.*

Caramel Corn

FARM KID fun

Kids love farms. That's just a fact. The animals are fascinating, the tractors are awe-inspiring, and the atmosphere is just plain fun. These kid-friendly foods will be enjoyed by junior farmers everywhere, whether they live in the country, the city, or somewhere in between.

Make this meal for a child's birthday party, or anytime you feel like having some good, old-fashioned farm fun. This is a great menu for the kids to make with Mom and Dad, or Grandma and Grandpa – imagine the fun you'll have building the barn and creating the farmyard scene on this yummy cake.

Go ahead ...
play with your food!

Chicken Feed Snack Mix

Chicken Feed Snack Mix

Prep: 12 minutes   Bake: 20 minutes

- ¼ cup apple jelly or desired-flavor jelly
- 3   tablespoons sugar
- 2   tablespoons butter or margarine
- ½   teaspoon ground cinnamon
- 1   cup rolled oats
- ½   cup peanuts or slivered almonds
- ¼   cup shelled sunflower seeds
- ¼   cup coconut
- 1   cup candy-coated peanuts

1. Preheat oven to 325°F. In a medium saucepan stir together jelly, sugar, butter or margarine, and cinnamo[n] Cook and stir over low heat until but[ter] or margarine melts and sugar [is] dissolved. Stir in the oats, peanuts almonds, sunflower seeds, and coco[nut] until combined.

2. Pour the mixture into an ungreas[ed] baking pan. Spread the mixture in [an] even layer. Bake in the preheated ov[en] for 20 to 25 minutes or until ligh[t] browned, stirring once or twice.

3. Transfer mixture to a large pi[ece] of foil; let cool. Store in a cove[red] container in a cool, dry place for u[p to] 2 weeks. (An airtight container will k[eep] the mixture crisp.) Just before serv[ing] stir in candy-coated peanuts. Ma[kes] 5 cups.

Fruit-Filled Feed Sacks

Spiral Silos

Start to Finish: 10 min.

Lettuce, mushrooms, and tomatoes make these wraps tops for kids. Tortillas come in an assortment of colors and flavors, which adds to the fun.

- 2 7- to 8-inch tomato-basil, spinach, and/or plain flour tortillas
- ¼ cup dairy sour cream, or ranch or chive dip
- 4 slices very thinly sliced cooked beef, chicken, turkey, or ham (about 2 ounces)
- ½ cup shredded lettuce
- ¼ cup finely chopped mushrooms
- ¼ cup finely chopped tomato

Spread each tortilla with 2 tablespoons of ranch or chive dip. Layer each tortilla with beef, chicken, turkey, or ham. Top with lettuce, mushrooms, and tomato. Roll up tightly. Trim off uneven ends. Cut each roll into 4 pieces. Stack slices to look like silos. Makes 8 slices.

Fruit-Filled Feed Sacks

Start to Finish: 10 min.

- ¾ cup cut-up strawberries
- 3 cups cut-up fruits, such as apples, bananas, pitted cherries, seedless red grapes, kiwifruit, and/or peaches
- 6 large waffle cones

Place strawberries in a blender; cover and puree until smooth. Place apples, bananas, cherries, grapes, kiwifruit, and/or peaches in large bowl, and gently toss together. Spoon into cones. Drizzle with the strawberry puree. Makes 6 servings.

Moo Juice

Start to finish: 10 min.

This utterly fantastic party refresher whips quickly in the blender. Part of the fun can letting kids choose their favorite flavor.

- ½ gallon vanilla ice cream
- 2 cups vanilla-flavored, strawberry-flavored, or chocolate-flavored milk

Place the ice cream and milk, half at a time, in a blender. Cover and blend until smooth, stopping to stir down several times with a rubber spatula, if necessary. Repeat with remaining ice cream and milk. Makes (4-ounce) servings.

Moo Juice and Spiral Silos

FARM KID *fun*

Pigs Under Wraps
Prep: 15 min. Bake: 12 min.

2   **tablespoons yellow mustard**
1   **tablespoon honey**
1   **11.5-ounce package (8) refrigerated corn bread twists**
8   **frankfurters**
     Finely shredded fresh Parmesan cheese

1. Preheat oven to 375°F. In a small bowl combine mustard and honey; set aside.

2. Unroll corn bread twists. Separate into 16 short strips. Gently flatten each strip; press pairs of strips together end to end, forming 8 long strips. Wind each dough strip around a frankfurter, leaving the frankfurter ends uncovered and stretching the dough as necessary. Lay wrapped frankfurters on a greased baking sheet. Brush with mustard mixture and sprinkle with shredded cheese.

3. Bake for 12 to 15 minutes or until bottoms are golden brown. Serve warm. Makes 8 servings.

Pigs Under Wraps

Sugar Cookie Farm Animals

Prep: 20 min. Bake: 7 min. per batch

⅔ **cup butter**
¾ **cup sugar**
1 **teaspoon baking powder**
¼ **teaspoon salt**
1 **egg**
1 **tablespoon milk**
1 **teaspoon vanilla**
2 **cups all-purpose flour**
2 **tablespoons unsweetened cocoa powder**
    Shredded wheat biscuits, crumbled
    Canned white frosting

In a large mixing bowl beat butter with an electric mixer on medium high speed for 30 seconds. Add sugar, baking powder, and salt. Beat until combined, scraping sides of bowl occasionally. Beat in egg, milk, and vanilla until combined. Beat in as much of the flour as you can with the mixer. Stir in any remaining flour. Divide dough in half. Knead the cocoa powder into one dough half. If necessary, cover and chill dough for 30 minutes or until easy to handle.

2. Preheat oven to 375°F. For cow cookies, on a lightly floured surface roll the plain dough until ⅛ inch thick. Place ½-inch balls of chocolate dough on the plain dough at 2-inch intervals. Roll lightly to flatten the chocolate dough (see photo below left). Use a 3-inch cow-shape cutter to cut dough. Place cutouts 1 inch apart on ungreased cookie sheets. For horses, roll remaining chocolate dough until ⅛ inch thick. Use a 3-inch horse-shape cutter to cut dough. Place cutouts 1 inch apart on ungreased cookie sheets.

3. Bake in preheated oven for 7 to 8 minutes or until edges are firm and bottoms are very lightly browned. Transfer to a wire rack and let cool.

4. To add manes and tails to the horses, attach the crumbled shredded wheat biscuits with canned frosting. Makes about 40 cookies.

FARM KID *fun*

Farmyard Cake
Prep: 1 hour

Using a frosted half-sheet cake purchased from a local bakery makes this kid-pleasing farm scene come together in half the time it would otherwise. Let this photo be your guide in creating a themed dessert that's almost too cute to eat.

Mixed nuts
1   purchased white-frosted halfsheetcake (about 15×11-inch)
    Shredded coconut
    Green food coloring
    Blue colored sugar (optional)
    Graham Cracker Barn
    Sugar Cookie Farm Animals
    Pretzel sticks
    Shredded wheat biscuits, crumbled

1. Press mixed nuts into sides of cake. (If frosting has dried, brush sides of cake lightly with water to moisten.) Place coconut in a resealable plastic bag or a bowl. Add food coloring. Knead the bag with your fingers to evenly tint the coconut. Sprinkle coconut over cake. If desired, sprinkle blue colored sugar for a pond.

2. Arrange Graham Cracker Barn and Silo on the cake. Place the Sugar Cookie Farm Animals on the cake. For fencing, stand crisscrossed pretzel sticks at 1- to 2-inch intervals; lay pretzel sticks across the V shapes. Use shredded wheat biscuits to make hay stacks. Makes 25 servings.

Graham Cracker Barn and Silo
Prep: 55 min. Stand: 3½ hours

Once you've cut the crackers as directed, refer to our how-to photos below and opposite to assemble the barn and silo. Be sure to let the frosting dry the entire time that's specified so that your structures will remain upright.

14   graham cracker rectangles (plus extras for breakage)
 3   8¼-inch pretzel rods
 1   cup sifted powdered sugar
 1   cup canned vanilla frosting
 1   4-inch cardboard tube (1½ inches in diameter)
 1   plain cupcake
     Canned vanilla frosting
     Chocolate sprinkles
     Thin wheat crackers (32 to 40)
     Chocolate graham cracker (optional)
     Pretzel sticks (optional)

1. Cut the silo and barn pieces. With a small serrated knife, gently saw lengthwise through the center of 4 graham crackers along the perforations (you will have one extra piece). From 2 more crackers, cut the barn roof support sections using the pattern opposite (you will not use the trimmings). Gently saw ¾ inch from a short side of 2 more graham crackers, making two 3½-inch-long crackers (you will not need the ¾-inch pieces). Cut 2 pretzel rods into 2¼-inch-long pieces (you will have leftovers). Set all pieces aside.

2. Make the frosting. In a small bowl stir together powdered sugar and the 1 cup canned frosting until combined. Transfer mixture to

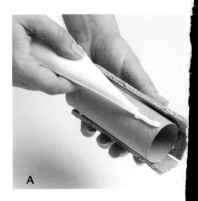

A

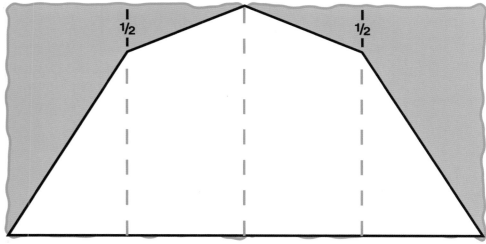

Barn Roof Support Sections
(Cut 2)

sturdy resealable plastic bag. Snip off a small portion of one corner. Or, spoon frosting mixture into a pastry bag fitted with a small round tip.

3. Assemble the silo. Pipe a line of frosting down the side of the cardboard tube (see photo A). Press a lengthwise-cut cracker section into place, flat side in. Repeat with 4 more sections to cover the tube. For the dome, cut the cupcake horizontally in half (you will not use the bottom half). Frost top half with additional canned vanilla frosting. Coat with chocolate sprinkles. Place on top of the silo. Set silo aside to dry for about ½ hours.

4. Assemble the barn. With flat sides up, lay a whole graham cracker next to the straight edge of a roof support section to form the barn front. Pipe frosting on a 3½-inch graham cracker and lay the cracker on the barn front to hold the pieces together (see photo B). Repeat to make the barn back.

On the barn front, pipe lines of frosting on the whole graham cracker's short edges; press 2¼-inch pretzel rods into the piped frosting. Pipe lines of frosting on the outside edges of the pretzel rods; press whole graham crackers into the pretzel rods with flat sides in to make the walls. Hold the walls in place with glasses, as shown (see photo B). Let the front and back barn units dry for about 1½ hours.

When dry, place the barn units upright. Attach the barn back to the walls with piped frosting and the remaining 2¼-inch pretzel rods as before. Pipe frosting along the roof line, and press two lengthwise-cut cracker sections into place to form the peak of the roof (see photo C).

Use the remaining two whole crackers to complete the roof. Pipe another line of frosting along the peak of the roof and press the whole pretzel rod into place.

5. Decorate the barn. "Shingle" the roof by piping lines of frosting onto the roof and pressing thin wheat crackers in place (see photo D). If desired, make a barn door by attaching sections of a chocolate graham cracker to the barn front with frosting. Outline the door by attaching pretzel sticks with piped frosting. Makes 1 barn and 1 silo.

B

C

D

Index of Recipes